Samuel SMEDLEY

Samuel SMEDLEY
CONNECTICUT PRIVATEER

JACKSON KUHL

Charleston · London

THE
History
PRESS

Published by The History Press
Charleston, SC 29403
www.historypress.net

Front cover images: © William D. Lee.

First published 2011
Manufactured in the United States
ISBN 978.1.60949.228.1

Library of Congress Cataloging-in-Publication Data

Kuhl, Jackson.
Samuel Smedley : Connecticut privateer / Jackson Kuhl.
p. cm.
Includes bibliographical references and index.
ISBN 978-1-60949-228-1
1. Smedley, Samuel, 1753-1812. 2. Ship captains--United States--Biography.
3. Ship captains--Connecticut--Biography. 4. United States--History--Revolution,
1775-1783--Biography. 5. United States--History--Revolution, 1775-1783--Naval
operations. 6. Connecticut--History--Revolution, 1775-1783. 7. Privateering--United
States--History--18th century. 8. Fairfield (Conn.)--Biography. I. Title.
E207.S64K84 2011
974.6'03092--dc22
[B]
2011015494

For Kristie.

CONTENTS

Acknowledgments

This book would not have been possible without the assistance and cooperation of everyone at the Fairfield Museum and History Center, who have always been so kind and generous to me. In particular, I am indebted to Rod MacKenzie and his encyclopedic knowledge of Fairfield history; Walter Matis, for his wonderful conversations and insight into the time period; and Barbara Bryan, for her help.

William Lee was incredibly gracious in supplying art for the book—I cannot thank him enough. The Fairfield Public Library and the Pequot Library, for this and countless other projects, have been invaluable sources for research. I am also indebted to Joseph Avitable, for information about Connecticut's maritime trade; Tom Crudbeard, for answering a technical question about cannons; Sierra Dixon and Richard Malley of the Connecticut Historical Society; Tricia Royston of the New London County Historical Society; Robert Kranyik of the Fayerweather Yacht Club; the Connecticut State Library, State Archives; the South Carolina Department of Archives and History; the William L. Clements Library, University of Michigan; Baylen Linnekin, for his encouragement; and Jeffrey Saraceno at The History Press, for his assistance. Finally, a big thank-you goes to friends and family, for their support—most of all to my wife and sons.

Chapter 1

"TWO CAN PLAY AT THIS GAME"

NORTHEAST OF THE LESSER ANTILLES, 1778—

Captain Dike snapped shut his spyglass. Off the stern rail, rolling water replaced his magnified vision—not the deep gray-green of the North Atlantic but the warm indigo of the almost Caribbean, a seascape broken only by sails. Two sets of sails, about six miles off, making directly for the *Cyrus* and the *Admiral Keppel*.

And overtaking them. Through his telescope, Dike had seen the pursuers flying a Continental flag, a mix of blue and white unfamiliar to him but doubtless belonging to the American rebels. They made better time against the two English ships, both out of Bristol fully loaded with cargoes of dry goods and painters' colors, hats and shoes, plus several passengers, bound for the colonies at St. Kitts and Jamaica.

Just as well. Dike and countryman Captain Brown of the *Admiral Keppel*, sailing in tandem, had been hoping for such an opportunity. There was money to be made in running wares to the West Indies, yes, but for them, it was just ordinary money—salary money. More money was to be made bringing in prizes: capturing Continental ships and selling the vessels and their cargoes at auction. Half of the profits would go to Mr. Hound, owner of the *Cyrus* and the *Admiral Keppel*, but the rest would be divvied into shares for officers and crew. This was on top of their regular wages. The *Cyrus* and the *Admiral Keppel* were letters of marque—ships whose primary duty was running cargo but also had permission to engage the enemy.

The difference between having a privateering commission or not was a noose. If a captain didn't have a letter of marque and attacked a ship, he was a pirate. Pirates were hanged. And, of course, no court would award a prize to a pirate. But if he overcame a ship while possessing a letter of marque, the admiralty court would judge the prize his lawful possession. And if the captain lost the fight and was captured, he and his crew were treated as prisoners of war, to be held until they were exchanged or hostilities ceased.

Dike ordered his men to raise the French flag atop the mainmast. All ships carried the flags of various nationalities aboard, flying different ones according to the circumstances. Having revolted against Parliament and crown, opinion among the Americans naturally turned favorably toward England's arch-nemesis. And, in fact, unknown to Dike, the two Continental ships had come upon a French ship late the previous afternoon, out of Santo Domingo, returning home. The French captain had been invited aboard for dinner, where he shared the news of having passed the two southbound English ships. To the Continentals, this was welcome information. They returned their guest to his vessel, bid him bon voyage and set course in pursuit of the Englishmen.

Up *Cyrus*'s pole went the French flag. Dike's plan was to let the Americans think the two English ships were friends, not enemies, and lure them into range of the cannons. Once they realized their mistake, it would be too late. Either the rebels would strike their colors—that is, indicate surrender by lowering their flag in submission—or they would receive the first cannonade.

The lead ship approached, about eighty feet long with sixteen guns. Dike could read the name *Defence* on its bow. A half mile off, Dike commanded the trap be sprung: down came the French jack, up went the Union crosses. It was too late for the Continentals to run.

"Where are you from?" Dike shouted across the span. "Where are you bound?"

The captain of the *Defence*, through the speaking trumpet, replied. "We are from Boston and we are on a cruise."

The Connecticut state ship *Defence* after its conversion from a two-masted brig into a three-masted ship. *William D. Lee.*

"Then," called Dike, "haul down them colors or I will sink you!"

Dike could hear the hooting and laughter of the other captain and his men. "There is time enough for that yet," came the response. "Two can play at this game, you must know!"

Dike shook his head—American yokels, too drunk on rum and pamphlet rhetoric to have any sense. Well, a few cannonballs would teach them the error of defying the king. Dike gave the order to fire.

Sailors put slow matches to powder, and eight cannons leapt back on their carriages, straining their breeching ropes, roaring with sound and smoke.

Captain and crew of *Cyrus* squinted through the sulfurous fog blowing into their eyes, eager to see what toothpicks remained of the other ship.

Then, across the water, they heard a collective cheer, then another and then a third. The smoke washed away, and Dike could see clearly: sky showed through rips in *Defence*'s sails but not a pinhole had been shot into hull or sailor. *Cyrus* had overshot.

Dike swore. The other ship approached from upwind. *Cyrus* was leeward, heeled over by the breeze. Their cannons on the windward side, the side facing *Defence*, pointed up—too high.

The men hauled on the train tackles, scrambling to pull the guns back in and reload; they were wide open to a retaliatory broadside. Singing carried across from the *Defence*. Dike recognized the tune and was amazed. Didn't these American rustics know that "Yankee Doodle" was an English song mocking them?

Further ahead, the other American ship—the *Oliver Cromwell*, of all names—closed with the *Admiral Keppel*. One hundred yards from her, *Oliver Cromwell* fired a bow cannon. *Admiral Keppel* responded likewise off the stern. Still the *Oliver Cromwell* inched forward, coming close to the Britisher's portside quarter.

Defence refused to fire at the *Cyrus*, instead straining every inch of canvas to pull even and then ahead. The ships jockeyed for raking position, each trying to move past, then cross the other's bow to force the other to reduce speed and turn. Dike cursed and screamed at his men to adjust their aim. Sailors stabbed handspikes under the butts of the cannons, thrust wooden wedges underneath so the muzzles pointed lower. Hit them this time. Hit them now!

Cyrus fired again. Plumes of water erupted in the ocean between the two ships. Still *Defence* was unscathed. Now *Cyrus* had undershot. *Defence*'s gunners had already adjusted for the tilt of aiming downwind, their cannons leveled at *Cyrus*—because they had done it before. For Dike, it was one thing to carry a letter of marque in his pocket, but it was another entirely to be a privateer.

Defence gained. The two ships stood parallel, the waves leaping between them as they raced.

And then *Defence*'s cannons spouted flame, launching six pounds of 96 to 98 percent iron, 2 to 4 percent carbon and silicon through the air at 545 miles per hour, as fast as the cruising speed of a Boeing 747. Times eight.

The shot ripped through *Cyrus*, through rope and wood and sailor. Within seconds, men sprawled upon the decks, dead and broken. The rudder wheel vanished, blasted into splinters. The ship was uncontrollable.

Still *Defence* pressed forward, well ahead of the now foundering *Cyrus*. At the captain's orders, men hurried to furl the fore-topsail, reducing *Defence*'s speed. She banked, presenting her side to *Cyrus*'s bow—another broadside.

Foremasts tumbled from above like felled trees, carrying down rigging and spars with them, smashing everything below. *Defence* came around and ran alongside. Nimble as monkeys, marines leapt from rail to deck, cutlasses and axes in hand.

They found no resistance. Nine of *Cyrus*'s thirty-five men lay dead, others wounded, the rest "horribly panic struck." Captain Dike surrendered instantly.

Later, the *Defence* would rendezvous with the *Oliver Cromwell*, some two hours' sailing away. They, too, had caught their prey, although they had a harder time of it, exchanging broadside after broadside: two dead, six wounded, their captain of marines mortally wounded, the ship itself hulled nine times. *Admiral Keppel* had similar casualties; their main mast was snapped by a nine-pound shot. Later still, the captains of the Continental ships would provide a long boat for Captains Dike and Brown and eleven others—including three female passengers—and point them toward St. Kitts. The rest were taken out of the *Cyrus* and the *Admiral Keppel*, clamped into leg irons and chained below decks, bound for Continental prisons. The prizes were manned with crews that would sail them north to Boston and the auctioneer's block. *Defence* and *Oliver Cromwell*, meanwhile, would make repairs. They would then head farther south into the Caribbean for more hunting, without result, before turning north again for Charleston, South Carolina.[1]

But before all of that, Captain Dike of the *Cyrus*, having struck his colors in submission to the Continentals, would have left the blood and splinters of his ship. He would have been brought onboard the *Defence* to formally offer his surrender and then to enjoy the courtesy between officers, perhaps to dine and converse with the opposing captain—to confront his enemy.

There is a story, without source and no doubt apocryphal, that when Captain Dike first met Samuel Smedley of Fairfield, Connecticut, he was shocked by his appearance. "There is little hope," Dike allegedly said, "of conquering an enemy whose very schoolboys are capable of valor equaling that of trained veterans of naval warfare."[2]

Captain Samuel Smedley was twenty-five years old at that moment in time, an adult, though possessing a round, baby face. And while behind that youthful countenance laid an incredible cunning, a brass daring and perhaps a revolutionary zeal matched by frustration with those who didn't share it, there was also a gentleman's manners and a great sense of fidelity. Smedley signed on to the Connecticut state ship *Defence* in 1775 as lieutenant of marines. In less than a year, he was her captain. Over his career, he would capture or aid in capturing more than a dozen prizes, survive shipwreck, battle Loyalists off the shores of his hometown, twice captain privateers and twice be captured by the British, escape the infamous Mill Prison in England and sail victoriously, at war's end, back to the newly independent country he so strenuously loved.

Chapter 2

"A CONNECTICUT MAN BORN"

The stretch of the King's Highway running eastward from Norwalk was stony and poor. To reach downtown Fairfield, Samuel Smedley would have first had to ride along the highway north, away from Long Island Sound into the hills, until it came to the ford across a neck of the Mill River. There was no bridge. From there, the highway turned south again along the riverbank and then east into town. There were eight miles between the two communities as the crow flies but twelve miles of road.

The highway would have then led Smedley into Fairfield's center. At the intersection where the road turns southeast for a thousand feet, he would have passed the house of his older brother, John. There he would have turned the corner, nudging his hired horse along the dirt-packed street toward the Trinity Church—the town's Anglican Church—at its foot. He would have ridden past the houses of his neighbors: Francis Forgue, the French doctor who had petitioned the Connecticut Assembly for permission to dwell in the colony; and Andrew Rowland, uncle to his wife. He would have passed a stone marker indicating sixty-three miles to New York, also the exact same mileage to Hartford. And finally, where the road turned in a sharp right angle to the northeast, he would have seen one last house on the corner, with a broad wraparound porch and a low, dormered second story capped by a mansard roof. Home.

The house actually belonged to his wife, Esther. Samuel was eighteen years old when he married into one of the most influential families in the town. Esther Rowland was the daughter of David Rowland: deputy, justice, judge in both the county court and the Fairfield Probate Court. After his death, David's younger brother, Andrew, filled most of those same roles and became the state's attorney for Fairfield County. Esther's mother, Elizabeth, was David's second wife. She died of dysentery in the summer of 1753, when "the bloody Flux raged to such a degree that 2 or 3 were buried in Fairfield daily." She was twenty-seven, her daughter less than two years old.[3]

Samuel had an upbringing not unlike that of his wife. His mother, Mary, was also his father's second spouse; likewise, she didn't live long enough to see him grown and wed, though her passing occurred at a riper age. (She was forty-four when she had him.) His father, James, was highly regarded, having risen to the rank of lieutenant colonel fighting, and being injured, in the French and Indian War. James had two surviving children from his first marriage to Jane Sturgis, daughter of another Fairfield dynasty; these were Samuel's half siblings: John, nineteen years his senior, and Abigail, who married a boy from the prosperous Jennings family. The colonel died the same night Samuel and Esther's first daughter was born in November 1771. The girl, named for her mother, may have been premature, born less than seven months after their marriage and living only a few days. The couple faced a similar heartbreak three years later when Elizabeth was born, only to pass soon after.[4]

But on that spring day in 1775, Samuel Smedley would have ridden up the drive to the main house, dismounted his horse and handed the reins to his slave, York. Behind Smedley lay a hard 160 miles to Philadelphia.

The events of Concord and Lexington reverberated through the colonies, spread by Smedley and others like him. When the news had reached Fairfield in April 1775, Smedley had been dispatched along with three others to Hartford and then to Philadelphia, where the delegates to the second Continental Congress were beginning to collect. Upon his return, Smedley expensed the costs for the horses' shoeing and hire (three pounds, five shillings, nine pence) to Fairfield. The town paid because the premiere families of Fairfield—and therefore the town itself—were firmly on the side of revolution.[5]

If Smedley had, on the morning after his return, stepped outside his home and continued his journey east along the King's Highway, he would have passed several widely spaced houses, including that of Thaddeus Burr. Burr was a distant cousin of his mother's and a good friend to the president of the Continental Congress, John Hancock—such a good friend, in fact, that four months hence Hancock would marry Dorothy Quincy in that same house. And further down the road, Smedley would have passed the town prison, raised in 1768 after the old gaol burned during an escape attempt by one of its occupants, and the gaol keeper's house with its garden, behind which Smedley would have spied the shallow pond where they dunked accused witches in the previous century. Then the Meeting House Green would have come, with the new courthouse on the right-hand side; on the left, Christ's Church; and beyond it, the little schoolhouse where Smedley had learned his sums and differences. Farther east, another road split away from the highway, and by following it, Smedley would have come to a corduroy road along the edge of a marsh, through the reeds and salt hay and past Peter Penfield's tide mills and then across the bridge over the Ash-House Creek into Black Rock. On his right would have been Grover's Hill. The road would have taken him over the shoulder of the hill, and as he

A mural of Black Rock Harbor as it appeared in 1808, the year the first lighthouse was built on Fayerweather Island. The mural, painted by Robert Lambdin, was placed inside the Black Rock Bank on the corner of Fairfield Avenue and Brewster Street in 1948. *Fairfield Museum and History Center.*

crested it and started down the slope, he would see a forest of masts and rigging before him: Black Rock Harbor, just two miles from Smedley's home—the real heart of Fairfield.[6]

The harbor is deep and wide and perfectly made for commerce, shielded from the Sound by a skinny, mosquito-ridden barrier beach called Fayerweather Island. In the harbor, Smedley would have seen brigs and brigantines, schooners and ships, some surrounded by smaller tenders lading and unlading cargo, landing it on shore or taking it out to the vessels. Others lay tied alongside the multiple wharves, with stevedores rolling casks down their gangplanks and up the pier to the warehouses. Seagulls cried, supercargoes barked directions. Perhaps that particular day Smedley would have seen the produce of Connecticut, bound for the French West Indies: wooden planks, barrel staves and hoops, potatoes, onions and horses—dozens and dozens of horses, along with the hay and oats to feed them. Hogsheads of pork, corn, cheese and onions would have been loaded for direct shipment to the rest of New England and New York. And maybe Smedley would have seen a foreign trader or two as well—from the Netherlands perhaps—unloading linen and tea. All of it was a reason for Fairfield's success as a town and the reason for much of the revolutionary zeal of its citizens—because all of it was illegal.[7]

Common Liquid Measurements Used in Eighteenth-Century America

Barrel	A wooden container holding 31.5 gallons.
Hogshead	A cask containing 63 gallons, the equivalent of two barrels.
Puncheon	A cask containing about 80 gallons.

The southern American colonies grew things farmers could not grow in England: cotton, tobacco, rice and indigo. But in New England, farmers produced many of the same things as their fellows in Britain, like wheat and cattle. Even though the colonies existed for the material support of the mother country, protectionist laws benefiting English farmers mostly prevented New Englanders from selling their goods there.

And because the Acts of Trade and Navigation outlawed the export of most commodities to non-English ports (even Scottish and Irish ports were forbidden), New England traders found themselves in a cul-de-sac. Further exacerbating the problem was that Americans greatly desired English-manufactured goods. But without markets for their produce, they couldn't afford them. In 1765, the colonies exported an estimated £1.5 million worth of goods to Britain but imported £2 million. That difference had to come from somewhere.[8]

On the edge of the Revolution, 50 percent of Connecticut's exports went to the Caribbean. The islands of the West Indies cultivated one major crop: sugarcane, which they sold within their respective empires as sugar, molasses and rum. But the Indies' single-minded focus meant they were unable to sustain themselves. They lacked foodstuffs to feed the slaves working the fields; they lacked the beasts of burden to turn the millstones and carry the results to market; they even needed the staves and hoops to construct the barrels to hold the molasses and rum. Here was the marketplace New England demanded, especially meat and livestock: Connecticut's top exports in 1770 were horses, beef, pork and cattle. And while Connecticut traders were sending most of their cargoes to British plantations, they were also selling them (as much as 40 percent of the trade) to islands held by foreign powers, whose own mercantilist laws further intensified shortages. French ports in particular welcomed New England vessels. France prohibited the importation of rum to protect their indigenous brandy market, and so the French island plantations had no legal outlet for their liquor beyond what they themselves could drink.[9]

Return cargoes of sugar, molasses and rum fetched good prices in Connecticut. Molasses in particular could be sold to distilleries in Rhode Island and Massachusetts to make high-quality rum, thus becoming a segment of the triangular slave trade. Yet the duties lay upon the three commodities—which, in the words of one historian, "were intended to be regulative and not revenue-producing"—which encouraged their landing far from the eyes of customs collectors.[10]

Most of the remainder of Connecticut's exports went to neighboring colonies. But here again, Connecticut merchants ran afoul of Parliament's shortsightedness. While the infrastructure for shipping in Black Rock was legal, the harbor had no customs collector nor was it designated a legal

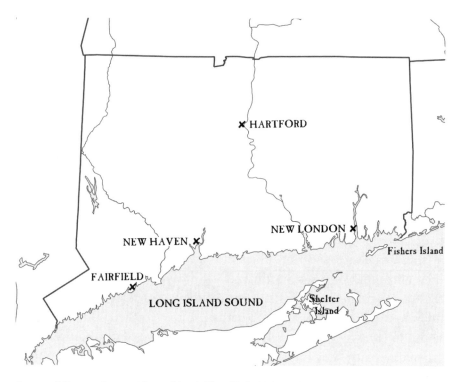

A map of Connecticut and Long Island, New York. *Jackson Kuhl.*

port. Just prior to the Revolution, Connecticut had only two legal ports: New London and New Haven. This meant that all maritime commerce was supposed to flow through either of those two cities. So if Fairfield traders wanted to sell goods to, say, Smithtown, Long Island—lying within sight of Fairfield, directly across the Sound—they first had to cart or ship their goods twenty-two miles up the coast to New Haven, post bonds, obtain paperwork and then sail back westward to their destination. This raised expenses and caused delays.[11]

Some Fairfield merchant captains may have obeyed these onerous rules. But there's little proof to think everyone did. With such a well-developed harbor, there weren't many practical reasons for a Fairfield ship to stop into New Haven or New London. Between the shipyard and the chandlery, if a captain needed a new sail, spar or mast, he could buy it in Fairfield; the workers and the warehouses existed in Fairfield to load and unload cargo. And though the 1733 Molasses Act taxes of nine pence per gallon of rum and six pence per gallon of molasses had long since been reduced, Connecticut sailors had evaded paying customs for so long that it's difficult to imagine they would have suddenly seen the error of their ways and begun funneling their shipping through the two legal ports.[12]

Of course, what really would have set a British official's teeth gnashing was the presence of a Dutch trader in Fairfield. The Navigation Acts proscribed foreign merchants from selling directly to Americans; most foreign goods were supposed to be imported to England first and from there exported to the colonies on British ships crewed by a majority of English sailors. But again, American demand overruled compliance. Patriots might boycott English tea, for example, but they held no such prejudices against the stuff off Dutch vessels.[13]

The head of the harbor near Ichabod Wheeler's shipyard, where the denuded ribs of a half-built vessel swarmed with carpenters as it lay on the ways, was Smedley's destination. This was the Upper Wharf. Built less than fifteen years prior, the wharf had been financed by a party of six investors. One of these had been James Smedley. Another was Ebenezer Bartram Jr., husband to Sam Smedley's cousin. The chandleries, sheds and storehouses of the Upper Wharf, of the Middle and Squire Wharves too, of the ships and their cargoes, were all owned by friends and relations: people like Ebenezer's brothers, Job and Barnabas Bartram; Francis Forgue, the French doctor; Thaddeus Burr; plus more Burrs, more Wheelers and a host of Sturgeses, kin to James Smedley's first wife. Even Sam had skin in the game: in 1772, "because a suitable store for receiving goods & provisions is much needed," Samuel Smedley and Samuel Sturges opened the Upper Wharf warehouse to which the longshoremen rolled the barrels of rum and molasses just off the ships. An area map drawn around 1779 for the British adjutant general shows a pair of rectangular structures, one on the Upper Wharf and another beside an inlet of what is today known as Brewster's Cove, captioned "Smedly's Stores."[14]

It's not clear beyond his father's share in the Upper Wharf how exactly Samuel Smedley arrived in the maritime trade. Some of his letters suggest he had served on ships before the war. As a teenager, he may very well have sailed onboard vessels captained by his cousin-in-law, Ebenezer Bartram, who was twenty-one years older and already established in the

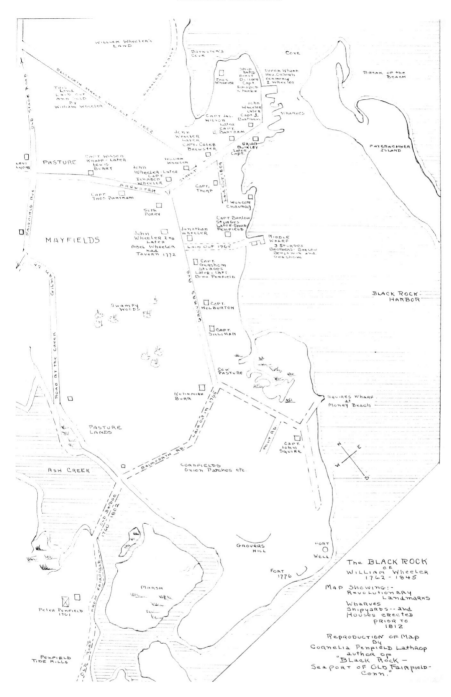

A detailed reconstruction of Black Rock Harbor prior to 1812. Reproduction of map by Cornelia Penfield Lathrop. *Fairfield Museum and History Center.*

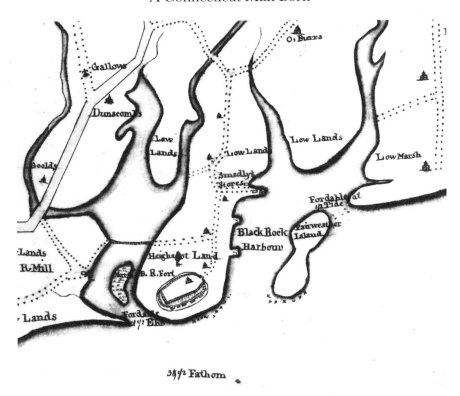

A map of Fairfield drawn by Andrew Skinner for the British adjutant general circa 1779. It shows the Upper, Middle and Squire Wharves of Black Rock Harbor, with "Smedly's Stores" on the Upper Wharf. *William L. Clements Library, University of Michigan.*

business. Most likely these voyages would have been to and from the West Indies. Smedley was simply a Fairfielder, a "Connecticut Man Born," and the people of Fairfield, Connecticut made their living off the sea. And the British, with their navigation acts and sugar tariffs, had not endeared themselves to the people of Fairfield.[15]

Resentment of the British only accumulated over the course of Smedley's second decade: first came George Grenville's Stamp Act in 1765, intended to pay down the debt of the French and Indian War. Every receipt, every bill of lading suddenly had a tax of four pence laid on it. Dozens of these papers passed through the hands of merchants every day. Petitions—like, say, to build a wharf or warehouse—cost one shilling, six pence; permission to grant the petition was six pounds. Court papers, a minimum of three pence each. Even for a sailor to walk into a dockside tavern and read the

A crumbling wharf in Black Rock Harbor. Although this particular dock may have been built in the nineteenth century, it rests on the Upper Wharf very close to one of "Smedly's Stores" shown on Andrew Skinner's map. Ichabod Wheeler's shipyard would have been where the woods are today. *Jackson Kuhl.*

An inlet off Brewster's Cove. The northernmost of "Smedly's Stores" would have existed on the left-hand shore. Low tide reveals the ruins of some structure, perhaps a pier for loading and unloading cargo. *Jackson Kuhl.*

news cost the tavern keeper at least twenty shillings for his license and the publisher a half to one penny per copy of his newspaper.[16]

The reply throughout Connecticut to the Stamp Act was "divers tumultuous and unlawful assemblies of persons, to the disturbance of the peace and terror of his Majesty's liege subjects." Mobs burned the stamp distributor, Jared Ingersoll, in effigy; pamphlets reviled both the act and Ingersoll. And though the assembly denounced the riots, they pursued revocation of the act. Smedley was intimately familiar with the details of the Stamp Act's repeal: his father-in-law, David Rowland, had been one of the three commissioners appointed by the general assembly to represent Connecticut at the congress to design its repeal in October 1765.[17]

But with repeal of the Stamp Act in March 1766 came the Townshend Revenue Act in its place, followed by its repeal; but of course, the tax of three pence per pound of tea remained. And then, in the wake of the Boston Tea Party, came the closing of Boston Harbor in June 1774. With nearly half of Connecticut's exports being the coastal trade—shipping to New York, Rhode Island and Massachusetts—the shuttering of a major port like Boston meant loafing on the docks of Black Rock. Throughout the colonies, from New York to Philadelphia to Virginia, assemblies condemned the closure, promising to organize what relief for Boston they could muster. Fairfield answered with 634 bushels of rye and 116 bushels of wheat: 750 bushels of grain total, donated from the people of Fairfield to the citizens of Boston "who are now Suffering under the Cruel Rod of Ministerial Tyranny and Oppression."[18]

What followed next were the events at Lexington and Concord, war with Britain and a complete disruption in trade.

For some sailors, this was an opportunity—work for idle hands.

Chapter 3

"FOR THE DEFENCE OF THE SEA-COASTS"

The final meetings in December 1775 of the Connecticut Assembly resulted in sheaves of legislation: acts for the raising and equipping of militia, for gunpowder manufacture, for the arrest of Loyalist saboteurs and the punishment of deserters. Throngs of officers were commissioned. Included in these were provisions for the safety of Connecticut's hundred-mile-long coastline.

The assembly had first addressed the issue back in July. Resolving "that two vessels of a suitable burthen be immediately fitted out and armed... for the defence of the sea-coasts in this Colony," the government hired "a certain brig, called the *Minerva*, belonging to Capt. Griswold and now lying in Connecticut River at Rocky Hill." Giles Hall was commissioned captain, the brig was fitted, a crew recruited. In October, *Minerva* was ordered on her first cruise.[19]

There was mutiny before they even left the harbor. "All the hands or soldiers and marines on board, except about 10 or 12, being duly noticed of said orders utterly declined and refused to obey the same and perform said cruise," Captain Hall testified to the assembly. No reasons were specified. The crewmembers may have been dissatisfied with the provisions or conditions on board, or perhaps they were nervous by the open-ended duration of the cruise (future orders from the assembly to the state ships usually defined the approximate length of the journey). To prevent the cancer from spreading, the entire venture was dissolved: the crew discharged, the guns and stores unloaded and *Minerva* returned to Griswold. The assembly was back to square one.[20]

Hall had been appointed to a committee to search for suitable vessels for the state's use. It may have been as a result of the committee's inquiries that the assembly came to learn of the *Lily Ann* owned by Captain John Griggs of Greenwich. It was a brig (a two-masted vessel rigged with square sails), almost new, having made only a single cruise to the West Indies. At sixty-two feet along the keel, twenty-three at the beam, it was perfect for a fighting ship. Rather than charter this one, however, the assembly decided to purchase it outright. The price tag was £1,000. And because it was resolved for the brig "to be fitted and improved as an armed vessel for the defence thereof," *Lily Ann* was rechristened with a more fitting nom de guerre.[21]

Defence was brought to New Haven for conversion from a cargo sailer to a warship. Captain Isaac Sears provided the cannons. Sears was a

A drawing of the ship *Defence*. Artist unknown. *Fairfield Museum and History Center.*

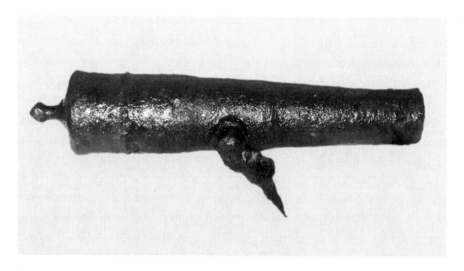

A cast-iron swivel gun believed to be from the 1779 Battle of Penobscot. Swivels were mounted on a ship's rails or gunwales. *Naval Historical Center Underwater Archaeology Branch.*

merchant and die-hard Patriot, a member of the Sons of Liberty in New York. In May 1775, he and his business partner, Thomas Ivers, loaned to New Haven and the colony sixty-six cannons of various gauges— weapons grabbed from the arsenal in New York City by a Sears-led mob in reaction to the news of Lexington and Concord. Fourteen of Sears's and Ivers's six-pound cannons (cannons were measured by the rough weight of the cannonballs they shot) went onboard the *Defence*. The brig mounted sixteen in all, supplemented by twelve to twenty-four swivel guns. These were smaller, more maneuverable cannons that could be operated by a single gunner, about four feet long and shooting half-pound shot, mounted on pivots along the bulwarks. Their purpose was antipersonnel.[22]

The cannons were free, but bills for everything else piled up: one "Diana" figurehead, payable to Ralph Isaacs of New Haven (four pounds, ten shillings); gilding and painting for said figurehead, along with painting and striping the brig, payable to Charles Burroughs of New Haven (five pounds, five shillings); a speaking trumpet (four shillings, six pence); a brass box compass (two pounds, fifteen shillings). Also included onboard were stinkpots: ceramic jars filled with rotten fish, potassium nitrate and sulfur, lit by a cow-tail wick. They were smoke grenades, dropped below decks on enemy ships to flush out recalcitrant opponents; the cost for two dozen was one pound.[23]

Another bill was for eleven yards of blue tammie (a kind of wool) and twenty-six yards of white tammie for the ship's flag (two pounds, two shillings, nine pence). Commonly, the maritime jacks of the Revolution consisted of thirteen alternating red and white stripes, with or without an overlying rattlesnake. The Continental navy flew the Grand Union flag, similar to the modern U.S. flag but with the crosses of St. George and St. Andrew in the canton. Because all these include the color red, *Defence* doesn't seem to have flown them. Instead, the *Defence* may have used an early version of the Connecticut state flag, with the seal of Connecticut—featuring grapevines and perhaps the motto *Qui transtulit sustinet* ("He who transplanted still sustains," a reference to the colony's founding by pioneers from the Massachusetts Bay Colony)—in white on a field of blue (or perhaps vice versa). Alternately, the flag could have resembled that flown by the privateer *Retaliation*, which had thin blue stripes on a white field and a single blue grapevine in a white canton. This flag is sometimes referred to as the "Connecticut privateer flag," but there was nothing exclusive to privateers about it; it was simply an early Connecticut flag created at a time when no single version had been agreed upon.[24]

The governor of Connecticut during the Revolution was Jonathan Trumbull. Born in 1710, he was raised in Lebanon, Connecticut, where his father owned an import business. After graduating from Harvard, Trumbull studied divinity to become an ordained minister. He began a trading business with his brother, but when the brother died on a voyage in 1731, Trumbull gave up preaching to move back to his hometown and dedicate himself to the family profession. In 1736, Trumbull was elected to the assembly, becoming speaker of the lower house four years later. When the Stamp Act was revoked in March 1766, Parliament asserted its right to govern and tax the colonies and even demanded the colonial leaders take an oath swearing to this submission. The then governor, Thomas Fitch, and four others agreed to do so (Fitch feared Parliament would revoke the Connecticut charter if he didn't), but most of the assembly, led by Jonathan Trumbull, by then elected to the upper house, and Deputy Governor William Pitkin, stormed out of the chamber. The five men were left to administer the oath to each other. Anger over the oath carried to the election later that year, resulting in Pitkin being elected governor and Trumbull deputy governor. When Pitkin died in office in 1769, Trumbull succeeded him. He continued as governor of the state; of the thirteen colonial governors, Jonathan Trumbull was the only one who sided with the Patriot cause.[25]

The general assembly still met and voted throughout the war, but the conflict in Connecticut was mainly prosecuted by Trumbull and his elite Council of Safety. This was a group of handpicked men whom the governor trusted. Membership varied—Thaddeus Burr served from 1777 through 1779; and Jabez Huntington, who captained a letter-of-marque in September 1776, was a longtime member—but each sitting of the council, often held at Trumbull's store in Lebanon, usually consisted of five to seven men. Together with Governor Trumbull, they ran the war in Connecticut. Almost all were members of the assembly, and like Trumbull, many of them were merchants and traders skilled in logistics and management, of moving commodities from point A to point B. Connecticut was sometimes called the "Provisions State" during the Revolution because of its ability to supply the Continental army and the war effort. This was due in great part to Trumbull and his executive circle.[26]

In late February 1776, Trumbull and the Council of Safety "took into consideration the affair of appointing captain and other officers for the brig *Defence* now lying at New Haven, and talked largely upon it." They commissioned Seth Harding as captain. Harding, a native Cape Codder, had worked for more than a decade as a merchant captain running the West Indies trade out of Norwich, Connecticut. He gave up the life of sea spray and rolling decks in 1771 to immigrate, along with his daughter and second wife, to Liverpool, Nova Scotia. There Harding owned a salmon fishery and became an upstanding member of the community: justice of the peace, court justice, representative to the province's general assembly. But he soon found his political opinions, which were still thoroughly New England, out of step with his adamantly Loyalist neighbors. He decided to return his family to Norwich. Along the way, a British captain confiscated all of the Hardings' family possessions on the grounds they were property of the enemy. The family rearrived in Norwich without possessions or prospects.[27]

Harding had not been forgotten by his old friends. The safety council soon found work for him supervising the building of a ship—the second half of the backbone of the state's armada. This vessel, which would become the *Oliver Cromwell*, was currently under construction in Saybrook. Harding was also hired for "going round the sea coast, to see about buying or building a ship"; perhaps he had been the one to inform the assembly about *Lily Ann*'s availability. Yet the shipbuilder was competent and didn't require micromanaging, and nosing about the docksides was not the most fruitful use of Harding's years of seamanship. Matching him to the *Defence* was perfect.[28]

Other roles needed filling. The council selected Ebenezer Bartram as first lieutenant, James Hopkins of Middletown for second lieutenant, Jonathan McCleave as master. For lieutenant of marines, they selected Bartram's wife's cousin, Samuel Smedley. This choice probably had less to do with nepotism than with filling the slots with recommendations the council could trust. The colony's commitments to fill General Washington's army, plus its obligation to recruit for Connecticut's own coastal fortifications, drained the wharves. They badly needed competent sailors to man the *Defence*—especially ones who wouldn't go sideways, as they had onboard *Minerva*.[29]

Smedley barely had time to load his boarding pistol before Hopkins dropped out, and Smedley was promoted to second lieutenant. Joseph Squire, whose granduncle owned Squire Wharf at Black Rock, replaced Smedley as lieutenant of marines.[30]

By late March 1776, preparations were almost complete except for a vital component: a full crew of 120. This was far more than was needed to sail; the extra men acted as gunners and boarders during engagements. Every time a prize was taken, part of the crew would go aboard and sail it into a friendly port. Harding needed a surplus so that each such division didn't weaken *Defence*'s performance in future engagements.

With enough hands to work the ship, Harding and company sailed to New London to recruit sailors off the docks. On April 10, *Defence* was ordered back to New Haven to take receipt of further tools of the trade—

eight swivels, four hundred swivel shot, one hundred 6-pound shot and 1,500 pounds of gunpowder—and then to proceed west to Stamford, recruiting sailors along the way.[31]

They didn't get that far. With the siege of Boston lifted in March, General Washington had departed Massachusetts for New York, arriving in mid-April. There he learned intelligence that the British fleet lying off Newport intended to blockade New London. This was bad news: many of his troops were currently embarking at New London on transports for New York; a blockade could imperil the army. Washington requested Commodore Esek Hopkins, admiral of Congress's first naval expedition, to patrol near the city and intercept any such attempt. Bolstering this suspicion was a battle Hopkins fought in the early hours of April 6 in Block Island Sound, when the twenty-gun Britisher *Glasgow* sailed seemingly out of nowhere and tore into the fleet, engaging with four different vessels, including Hopkins' flagship, the twenty-four-gun *Alfred*. Yet *Glasgow* managed to escape into Newport after killing ten and wounding fourteen with minimal casualties herself. Accordingly, on the fifteenth, Trumbull ordered Harding and *Defence* to cruise under Hopkins "against our enemies." However, the enemy kept to the Narragansett; a serious threat of blockade was still some nine or ten months in the future. With nothing happening, Hopkins released *Defence* and another Connecticut ship, the schooner *Spy*, from their commitment.[32]

Harding reverted back to his original orders of the tenth, proceeding west to New Haven and then farther to recruit along the coast. At Fairfield, they tied up in the harbor and set to work buying drinks and collecting signatures. By May, Harding reported he had about one hundred men, almost his full complement.[33]

From Black Rock Harbor, *Defence* sailed westward again toward Stamford. On May 12, Harding "espied a small sloop attempting to cross the Sound." For whatever reason, Harding was suspicious and brought the sloop alongside. The eight onboard claimed they were heading to New York for shad, but the answer didn't satisfy Harding. "On more strict Enquiry [I] found to my Satisfaction they were Tories from the Town of Redding in Fairfield County bound to long Island to join Peter Fairchild a Noted Tory who had fled to the Island before."[34]

Redding is an inland town about seventeen miles north of Fairfield. In early 1775, more than one hundred townsmen signed a covenant forming the Redding Loyalist Association. "We consider it an indispensable duty we owe to our King and Constitution, our country and posterity," they wrote in their agreement, "to defend, maintain, and preserve at the risk of our lives and properties the prerogative of the crown, and the privileges of the subject from all attacks by any rebellious body of men." Peter Fairchild was believed to be the ringleader—he owned the tavern where the association met. When the order arrived for Redding to muster its militia, the association members deserted their homes, including Fairchild, who escaped to the Loyalist bastion of Long Island.[35]

Neither Connecticut nor Long Island was monolithically Whig or Tory. But as the war began, people sifted across Long Island Sound like sticks and stones separating in water. Washington's loss in Brooklyn in August 1776 and the subsequent seizure of New York City by the British further magnified the exodus. Back in July, when the Declaration of Independence was read in Huntington, on Long Island's north shore directly opposite Norwalk, drums were struck, the Union flag replaced, an effigy of King George blown up, muskets shot and thirteen toasts drank. Yet once the British seized control of city and state, the citizens of Huntington "dismissed their committees, repudiated all acts of congresses and committees and professed loyalty to 'the lawful sovereign.'" It was in Huntington where Connecticut spy Nathan Hale came ashore and was soon captured. Huntington's rejection was mirrored by their neighbors in Smithtown and Southold, also on the north shore, as well as numerous towns throughout the island. When Loyalist William Tryon, the restored governor of New York, toured Long Island, he applied the oath of allegiance to eight hundred militiamen in Suffolk County alone.[36]

Being a Loyalist in Connecticut wasn't an easy experience. In January 1777, Ebenezer Hall, a Fairfield citizen, was dragged in front of Trumbull and the Council of Safety "by virtue of a precept from the civil authority, selectmen and committee of inspection of the town of Fairfield, as being a person dangerous and inimical to this and the United States of America." After being harangued by the governor, Hall "declared himself fully convinced of the justice of the American cause" and was allowed to post £1,000 bond and return to Fairfield on the condition he neither leave town nor correspond with the enemy. Isaac Tomlinson of Woodbury likewise had an epiphany before the council, declaring "he never before so well understood the state of the dispute or the measures taken to prevent the shedding of blood." He, too, was allowed to post bond and return home. They were lucky—or at least clever. Tories who couldn't post bond or were suspected as being too inimical to remain free were thrown in Newgate Prison, an abandoned copper mine. It was a place its inmates, confined inside the earth in darkness, heat and cold, simply called "Hell."[37]

What Harding had stumbled upon was the beginnings of an exodus, as Patriots and Loyalists crisscrossed the Sound in search of security. It wasn't just a one-way street. Following the Battle of Long Island, the Patriot representatives of New York resolved "that it be recommended to the inhabitants of Suffolk, Long Island, to remove as many of their women, children and slaves and as much of their livestock and grain to the main as they can." Meanwhile, the British army on the island seized all food and livestock "being the property of persons actually in rebellion, or who have deserted their habitations." Just as the Redding Loyalists fled to Long Island, Patriots escaped to Connecticut.[38]

Harding seized the Tory sloop, put Smedley and some men onboard it and ordered them to Long Island in pursuit of Fairchild. But he then thought better of it, recalled Smedley and returned to Fairfield with his eight prisoners and the commandeered sloop.[39]

There, Samuel Hawley, one of the eight prisoners and a resident of Redding, confessed to Harding and Jonathan Sturges, a justice of the peace. The transcription of the confession, "the most minute account we have yet been able to get of a horrid Plot formed by the Tories to cooperate with our Enemies to destroy the Country," was sent to Trumbull and his Council of Safety. Harding promised leniency to Hawley, who "disclosed the Affair Voluntarily without any Compulsion and altogether free and seems to rejoice that he is stop'd in his Course and appears to be much relieved from the Distress of Mind the Tories generally Labour under." Harding emphasized that "Hawleys Confession was profusely voluntary."[40]

As the confession was "a profound Secret not communicated even to my officers," the text of this "Scheme of the blackest dye" has disappeared from history. Fortunately, Hawley wasn't the only garrulous conspirator.[41]

John McKey of Norwalk later testified that on April 15, a Charles McNeill of Redding approached him, saying that a colonel in the British army had in his possession lieutenant's commissions for each of them. The British were galvanizing the Loyalists into a fifth column to be called the Royal Americans. Their first job was to construct an intelligence network that would relay information about Continental troops to the British. But it soon fell apart. In the predawn hours of May 11, McNeill woke McKey at his house in Norwalk. McNeill and four other Loyalists were on the lam from the tar buckets of their unsympathetic neighbors and needed McKey's help. McKey hid them and arranged for a sloop to carry them to safety on Long Island. This was the same sloop Harding had intercepted; McNeill and McKey were among the eight passengers.[42]

All of this greatly agitated Captain Harding. He hired a small sloop named *Discovery* (five pounds, six shillings), and with Smedley in command, "fit her with two swivels," thirty or forty men, and sent them off, along with one of the prisoners to act as guide, to capture Fairchild and other "Tory deserters that we heard lodged at such a place." He had a Loyalist write beforehand to Fairchild and arrange a rendezvous, "which it is hoped will afford Lieut Smedley a favourable opportunity to Seize him." Harding sent Smedley for the simple reason that he knew Fairchild. Peter Fairchild had served as second lieutenant (of the Second Company, Third Regiment) under Smedley's father, James, during the French and Indian War. Samuel Smedley had probably met Fairchild and could identify him on sight; perhaps Harding believed Fairchild would surrender peacefully if Smedley appealed to the Tory tavern keeper's memory of his old commanding officer.[43]

Smedley and *Discovery* returned without Fairchild or any other news. Harding then ordered Smedley to take another confiscated sloop, called the *Life Guard*, to patrol the western Sound. Harding wrote: "It is my opinion it will be highly serviceable to employ several small Cruisers in the Sound especially at the Westward to prevent the Collection of Tories on the Island and to prevent the escape of those who are collected there."[44]

Harding wanted to completely sever communication between Connecticut and Long Island. No vessels should be allowed to pass, he said, unless they carried official certificates attesting to their purpose. The general assembly agreed, not just for sailors crossing the Sound but for everybody in the colony. In July, they passed an act that any traveler who was not "well known and friendly" had to produce a pass signed by "some Congress, Committee of Safety or of Inspection, some magistrate, justice of the peace, general or field officer in the army" specifying his business. Officials had the right "to stop and examine such persons travelling without certificate as aforesaid, and unless he or they can give full satisfaction that he or they are pursuing their lawful business, and are friendly to the liberties and interests of the United American States," the official was bound by duty to arrest the traveler. To cross the Sound, applicants had to apply in person to Trumbull's Council of Safety for a pass.[45]

In the end, Harding's suspicions of the sloop netted twenty-six Tories. Samuel Hawley was granted leniency, but for all his penitence, he joined the British and was captured yet again. He repeated his act of contrition, whereupon he sat out the rest of the war. John McKey had his home confiscated (it was legal to seize Tory property and lease it for the colony's benefit) and did prison time, though eventually he was freed and his estate restored. Charles McNeill escaped custody and joined the British. As for the notorious Peter Fairchild, he was commissioned by Robert Rogers as a captain in the Queen's Rangers.[46]

Smedley and the rest were soon reunited with *Defence*—the confiscated sloops presumably turned over to state or local authorities for their benefit; there is no mention of them being sold as prizes—and they returned to New London by late May before departing for Boston. Along the way, Harding and his crew, still excited by Tory conspiracies, boarded a number of boats out of Block Island (Smedley "formed in his mind the judgment that they were not so friendly as they ought to be to the American cause"), then sailed around Cape Cod and put in at Plymouth for ballast. Harding was born in Eastham to a family originally from Plymouth, so this may simply have been an alibi for social calling. He and his officers paid a visit to his friend, Nathaniel Lathrop, a physician. There, Harding "invited his Lady to come on board and bring with her as many of her Friends as she could collect" for a tour of the brig. Mrs. Lathrop obligingly sent out invitations. At the appointed time on Saturday, June 15, Harding sent a boat to ferry his guests the mile and a half to *Defence*. The four women consisted of Mrs. Lathrop, Mrs. Warren, Mrs. Elizabeth Shaw and Shaw's sister visiting from Quincy, whose husband was currently representing Massachusetts at the Continental Congress in Philadelphia.[47]

"Since I arrived here, I have really had a scene quite novel to me," wrote Abigail Adams to her dearest friend, John, describing the jaunt.

> *She is a fine Brigg, Mounts 16 Guns, 12 Swivells and carries 100 & 20 men….No private family ever appeard under better Regulation than the Crew. It was as still as tho there had been only half a dozen, not a prophane word among any of them. The Captain himself is an exemplary Man, Harden his name, has been in nine Sea engagements, says if he gets a Man who swears and finds he cannot reform him he turns him on shoar. Yet is free to confess that it was a sin of his youth.*

And she added, "He has one lieutenant a very fine fellow, Smelden by name." Apparently Mrs. Adams was impressed by Smedley's charm, if not his name.[48]

The guests drank tea while the crew put on the show of a mock engagement, demonstrating how a prize was captured. Then the children danced on the quarterdeck while some sailors fiddled and played flute. "Every mark of Respect and attention which was in their power, they shewd us," she wrote. On their way back to land, *Defence* gave a thunderous salute to the ladies with their cannons. It was, said Mrs. Adams, "a ceremony I would have very readily dispenced with."[49]

It's worth considering where and when Harding took part in "nine Sea engagements." Like many of the men sailing under him, Harding never had formal naval experience. Perhaps it was a boast to impress Mrs. Adams and the rest of the ladies; maybe he included his petty confiscation of the Loyalist sloops in that number. On the other hand, he may very well have held a letter of marque as a merchant mariner during the French and Indian War. Certainly Harding seems to have had some knowledge of tactics based on what happened next.

Defence sailed the following morning, June 16, toward Boston. It was very foggy. A constant pulsing of cannon fire grew the farther northward they went. About two o'clock, the fog swept off. From the top of the mast, a watchman spotted a ship and a brig just inside Boston Harbor being hounded by four eight-gun schooners. Both sides kept a continual fire, with the schooners in retreat. The brig and the ship stayed put.

The wind was low, so it wasn't until sunset that *Defence* caught up with the schooners. Signals were exchanged; everyone was friendly. One of the captains, William Burke, came aboard and told his story.

The brig and ship were transports—part of a Scottish convoy, the Americans would later learn—whose members had become scattered by a storm. These two were the first to arrive outside the harbor, and now they waited for the rest to catch up. What they didn't know was that

A Plan of the Town and Harbour of Boston by J. De Costa, 1775, showing the preferred routes used by ships entering Boston Harbor, including the Nantasket Road. Facsimile of the original in the map collection of the Yale University Library. *Fairfield Museum and History Center.*

the British had evacuated Boston in March. Meanwhile, the schooners had been buzzing like wasps around the transports since eight in the morning. "Capt Harding requested of him how many men they had all lost," Smedley wrote afterward. Burke answered: not one. Harding "told them they had not been near enough."[50]

Well, said Burke, do you try?

I have already determined to take them both, said Harding.

Burke went back to his schooner, and *Defence* set off. At eleven o'clock at night, they approached the two British transports riding anchor in Nantasket Road, the name given to a channel threading around Boston Harbor's southern peninsula and past the harbor's islands to the city.

Harding adopted a direct approach. He sailed *Defence* straight between the two enemy ships, dropped anchor and demanded their surrender.

"What Brigg is that[?]" asked a major named Menzies aboard the ship, *George*.

"*Defence*," replied Harding. He didn't want to kill the major's men, but he would have his ship at all costs. Harding said again: strike your colors to America.

Menzies was apoplectic. "Ye rebels strike!" This was followed by a broadside.

Defence immediately returned fire. Cannonade after cannonade cracked the air, orange tongues of flame momentarily lighting the night, as the Connecticut ship blasted away to either side; the enemy vessels were only about 200 to 250 feet away. The Britishers pounded back, fourteen guns aboard the ship *George*, sixteen aboard the brig *Annabella*. But their cannons sat higher than those onboard *Defence* and, in the close quarters, couldn't draw a good bead on the Yankee brig. They sliced shrouds and punctured sails but inflicted little structural damage. The three banged away for almost two hours, the four schooners sitting off and watching, goggle-eyed.[51]

Finally the British cannons muted. Through the saltpeter gun smoke, the crew of *Defence* heard a cry: neither vessel could take any more. Both enemies struck.

"My Officers and Men behaved with great bravery," Harding informed Trumbull, "no Men could have outdone them."[52]

Aboard *Defence* there were no deaths, just nine wounded, including

Justus Jennings who lost a leg (his job was ship's clerk). Smedley confidently opined, "Our wounded is all like to recover soon." And *Defence* was still very much seaworthy, even though, commented Harding, "My Brigg is much damaged in her sails & rigging." The British fared much worse. They lost eighteen altogether, including Major Menzies; as many as sixty were wounded.[53]

The ships were troop transports, Scotsmen under the command of Colonel Archibald Campbell of the Seventy-first Regiment of Highlanders. The royal admiralty had ordered a number of vessels to cruise outside Boston and divert incoming British ships to Halifax, but *George* and *Annabella* had unknowingly slipped through the screen. Between the pair, *Defence* captured 210 prisoners: soldiers mostly, but also women and children—their families. The troops had enlisted for "10 to 12 Guineas" plus a promise of one hundred acres of land. They had come to squash the rebels and afterward settle down as their neighbors.[54]

That was Sunday. On Tuesday, a third ship appeared, making for the harbor. Another member of the scattered convoy, heading for what its captain and passengers still supposed was a British port. *Defence*—this time assisted by the schooners—caught up and captured it, too. In the face of overwhelming opponents, though, not a single shot was fired.

Chapter 4

"TO CRUISE AGAINST THE ENEMIES"

The Capt[ains] of the four schooners Dispute with each other," Harding wrote to Governor Trumbull at the end of June 1776. "One sais you did not fight and you did not fite and so they go on."[55]

The capture of the three British ships—*George* and the brig *Annabella*, plus the third transport, *Lord Howe*—was a bonanza of prisoners, materiel and most definitely prestige. Another 112 highlanders were taken along with the *Lord Howe*, making the total 322 souls deflected from warring, directly or in a supporting role, against America. Included in these were high-value prisoners Colonel Campbell and his officers. As a gesture of respect, their side arms were returned immediately after the engagement, and they were allowed to accompany Major Menzies's funeral procession through the streets of Boston. Afterward, Campbell was paroled in Reading, Massachusetts, where he lived comfortably for the rest of the year.[56]

In 1776, prisoners were just a side effect of combat; but as the war progressed, their capture would become an end in itself. When news reached Congress that imprisoned American general Charles Lee was maltreated by the British, Campbell was yanked from his cozy confines and thrown into the more dismal conditions of the Concord gaol as retaliation. Campbell had another use, too: in May 1778, he was exchanged for Colonel Ethan Allen, who himself suffered severely during his two years' incarceration.[57]

Because the three vessels were troop transports, they carried everything necessary for equipping infantry: fuses, small arms and bayonets; shoulder straps, gun straps and leather bullet pouches; knapsacks, tents and tent poles; canteens and camp kettles; and blankets, clothing and stockings. Washington immediately demanded the supplies, and John Bradford, the navy agent in Boston, requisitioned the items and sent them to the army at New York.[58]

That left the ships themselves and the question of how to divide the profits of their sale. Smedley underscored the insignificance of the schooners' participation: "My reason for mentioning so particular about the above scooners," he wrote to Trumbull after describing their lackluster performance, "is because they want to share equal with us in the prizes when it is the voice of almost all the people here they according to Wright should have but small part if any thing." First Mate Ebenezer Bartram reiterated this, saying the victory was due solely "by the brave activity of our worthy Captn who Behavd like ye Seaman Like ye Gentman & Like a man of honnor." Harding libeled for three-fourths each of the *George* and *Annabella* (suggesting he credited one of the schooners—perhaps Burke's—for some participation) plus "my purporshon of the Ship Lord How." Samuel Eliot Jr., Connecticut's agent in Boston, stressed to Trumbull, "It is absolutely necessary that two intelligent Persons who were onboard the Brig should attend the Tryall—3 days will make an amazing difference—there are many Claimants."[59]

Under Congress's rules, the structure of dividing prizes was the same for both the Continental and the state navies: one-third to the captors and two-thirds to the nation or state. The exception was captured vessels of war; in which case, as an incentive, the prize was divided fifty-fifty. And the three transports were most certainly captured vessels of war. Eliot and the schooner captains jockeyed with one another, scrambling to boost their claims so that the admiralty court might award them that extra sliver of the spoils. *Defence* was eventually granted its share in the three, but because of the bankrupt wartime economy, Bradford became insolvent, resulting in a "long & unhappy Lawsuit" between him and Eliot that came to nothing. Officers and crew never saw a pence.[60]

In the meantime, *Defence* stayed in Nantasket Road while Harding came into Boston. "Your worthy Commander is now sick at my house, where the best care shall be taken of him," wrote Bradford, the naval agent, to Trumbull. "His disorder was a violent Seizure of a Cold, he has had two physicians. They've given him an Emetic & taken some blood from him; this morning he is so much reliev'd, that I make no doubt he will be abroad tomorrow." He added: "if in the Interim any thing should appear which rolls our cruisers out, I shall endeavor to get the brig among them to share in the Emolument."[61]

There was another reason why *Defence* didn't come into Boston with its captain: *Annabella* had caught on some rocks soon after the battle, from which the Yankees struggled to free her. Then, ten sails had suddenly appeared cruising outside the mouth of the harbor: two frigates and eight transports—the balance of the Highland Fleet.

This was all the cure Harding needed. He left Bradford's—"He had a very Strong impulse he should take a prize," wrote the naval agent—and returned to *Defence*'s helm. Yet the British sensed something amiss, and by June 28, they had vanished, gone to the new rendezvous at Halifax. "I believe the prospect of taking any more prizes is over," Harding wrote.[62]

Harding waited reluctantly in Boston for further orders. When they were slow in coming, he departed in early July on his own judgment. "It was the opinions of all his friends that he could not justify himself in staying while the small pox was so prevalent in this place," wrote Eliot, "and so many on board the Brig liable to take the infection."[63]

Defence returned to Connecticut. On the way they stopped in Newport where, on July 13, a dispute between Smedley and the ship's surgeon, Gideon Wells, was arbitrated. The exact cause isn't specified in the resolution of the three judges—Ebenezer Bartram, Josiah Burnham and Joseph Squire—but after "hearing their Case fully Tried & Debated," the judges came to six unanimous decisions:

> *First unanimously it Does not Apper that Dr. Wells Intendd anything Hurtfull to Lieut Smedley*
>
> *2d Unanimously it Does not appear that Lieut Smedley intendd any hurt to Dr. Wells —*
>
> *3d Unanimously it Does Appear that Both parties Intendd it only as a Rhomance.*
>
> *4th unanimously it Does Appear that Dr. Wells applied to Ye Captn to have Lieut Smedley Broke for so Trifleing a thing as Rhomance.*

5th unanimously this Court is of Oppinnion that Dr. Wells Offerd not Only an Insult to the Commissiond Officers But to all Ye Officers on Board

6th Unanimously this Court has come to Ye following Resolution that Dr. Wells is to ask Lieut. Smedley' pardon & Dr. Wells To sign the Above Sentence of Court. Now for Ye future all Burid in Oblivion & never to be mentiond more.

Wells signed.[64]

It is difficult to parse out the exact offenses committed, though by the order of the resolutions, it's reasonable to imagine that Wells said something to Smedley, Smedley said something back, Wells asked Harding to have Smedley punished and when the captain refused, Wells insulted all the officers onboard. Regardless of who said what to whom (none of which was meant literally, as both agreed it was a "Rhomance," a fiction, something derogatory said in heat), clearly the court was trying to defuse a duel. This was common procedure at the time: two men would argue and agree to duel, and then friends and colleagues would cool them down prior to the appointment, usually by arranging some way for both to save face. Many more invitations to duels were offered and accepted than were ever actually fought. While a prisoner in Quebec, Ethan Allen agreed to act as the second for his British captor, an army captain who had agreed to duel a naval lieutenant over some insult; but the matter was resolved when the two men's superiors intervened. In this case, if it was a matter of disciplining one or both parties, Harding would have had a hand in events, but he was entirely absent. With the cruise coming to an end—and of course it being impossible to fight while at sea—the matter demanded conclusion before it reached pistols at dawn in some lonely field. The trial provided it, and though Wells was required to ask pardon of Smedley, the doctor had only to live onboard with the shame of it for twenty-four hours.[65]

Defence arrived in New London on July 14. The following day, Captain Harding met with Governor Trumbull and his council in what would be a crucial turning point in *Defence*'s history. There, the council excused Harding for leaving Boston, and together they discussed "directions about cleaning, graving and refitting, and about the men who are probably infected with the small pox."[66]

Harding may have been displeased with *Defence*'s handling as a warship, or she may have been damaged in more than just sails and rigging. Nevertheless, the brig was beyond rehabilitation to Harding's and the council's suiting. So they decided to replace her.

Earlier in the year, just before *Defence* had joined for a short time with the flotilla under Commodore Esek Hopkins in protection of New London, Hopkins had learned intelligence that the forts at Nassau in the Bahamas contained a large amount of "powder and warlike stores." More notably,

Esek Hopkins, first commander in chief of the Continental navy. *Library of Congress.*

this trove was said to be poorly defended and materiel was something the nascent American Revolution sorely needed. Hopkins meant to have it.[67]

His fleet set off, rendezvousing at Abaco on March 1. Two days later, Hopkins's marines and sailors landed at New Providence and raided the island's two forts, opposed only by a few desultory shots. By the end of the day, Hopkins was in possession of cannons, mortars and two-dozen barrels of gunpowder—so much stuff that they couldn't fit it all onboard their ships for the return voyage to America.[68]

No problem. Hopkins commandeered at least one vessel, a Bermudian-made sloop named *Endeavour*, lying in the harbor. They packed part of the haul into its hold, and *Endeavour* sailed northward with the fleet, coming to rest in New London where it was unladed.[69]

It idled there still by July. On the twelfth, the Continental Congress restored *Endeavour* to its rightful owner, Charles Walker, who seems to have been shanghaied along with his sloop. But Walker's luck didn't last. Trumbull and his council instructed their agent to negotiate with Walker for the sale of *Endeavour* and its swivels shot and so on. Yet they simultaneously laid an injunction against the sloop from leaving port.[70]

Walker seems to have had no choice except to agree to the sale—though at a price tag of £2,168.12s.5d., he came out well. The original *Lily Ann* cost £1,000.[71]

So, on August 2, Trumbull and the Council purchased *Endeavour* and ordered Harding to "immediately proceed to alter and fit up said sloop as an armed brigantine with the greatest dispatch," transferring "the masts, sails, rigging, guns and other implements and furniture of the brigantine *Defence* now under his command." The name was carried over as well. *Endeavour* became the new *Defence*.[72]

As for the old *Defence*, the brig bought from Captain Griggs of Greenwich was used as a guard vessel to protect New London Harbor for about a year before being bonded and fitted as a letter of marque by two venture capitalists. Although the brig remained state property, the Council of Safety resolved that the independent captain "shall well and faithfully execute his office and trust aforesaid according to the orders of Congress"—meaning he had to abide by the privateering rules laid down by the Continental Congress in April 1776. The distinction between privateers and Connecticut's navy were not always so sharp.[73]

The refitting of the new *Defence* didn't take long. By August 12, Samuel Squire in Fairfield was ordered to deliver "forty barrels of pork, forty barrels of beef, forty bushels of beans and peas, and forty bushels of Indian corn" to the brig, and Harding was commanded "to cruise against the enemies of the United American States as soon as fitted to sail, for the space of about eight weeks."[74]

This time, Harding embarked upon a different strategy than before. *Defence* sailed east into the Atlantic, where they soon found two hundred merchant ships en route to England—the Jamaica fleet, bound from the West Indies with the produce of the British plantations; two men-of-war accompanied them. *Defence* shadowed the convoy, biding its time, until the men-of-war veered off, having reached the limit of their orders. The merchant ships were on their own.[75]

Defence pounced. The first prize was *John*, a ship laden with sugar and rum; next came *Guinea Man*; and then a third, the twelve-gun *Sally*, which fought back before striking. All were sent into New London to be condemned, the vessels and cargoes sold and some of the prisoners— Captain Dunbar and passenger James Watt from *John* and Captain Jackson and the ship's surgeon, John Wright, from *Sally*—to be exchanged for hostage Patriots of equal rank.[76]

But *Defence* found it tougher to return to New London than it had been to go out. Two British frigates, thirty-two guns each, caught sight of *Defence* and sailed to intercept. Though Harding strained every inch of canvas, the frigates gradually crept closer, close enough in Block Island Sound to open up their bow guns. *Defence* turned her stern chase guns on them, and the three ships pounded back and forth, producing smoke and wasting shot without injury.[77]

New London rests on the west bank of the Thames River, three miles upstream from where it runs into the Sound. The city had long been the colony's major port—it had been the colony's only legal port until 1760. Because of this, at the beginning of the war, the governor and his council decided to fortify it by abandoning the original nine-gun battery along the riverbank and erecting a halo of fortified emplacements. Fort Trumbull was built on a rocky peninsula jutting into the river called Mamacock, on the west bank just south of town. Fort Griswold lay across the river on Groton Height. A third fort was installed on the tip of a peninsula, Winthrop's Neck, north of town, but was deserted after a year or two. Theoretically, the three forts, along with another in the town itself, would provide an impenetrable aegis of protection for ships in the harbor, raking enemies from every direction. In reality, the forts lacked men and materiel—the "fort" in New London's town square was nothing

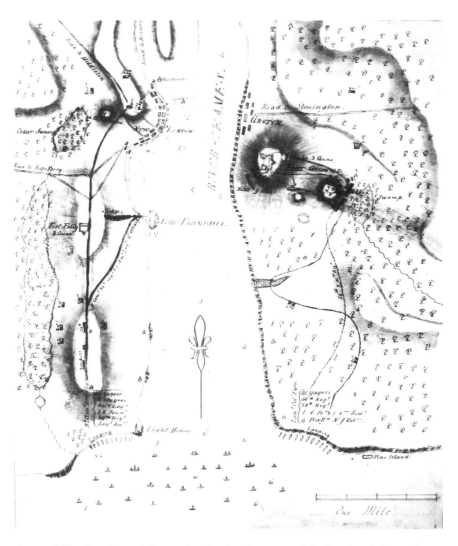

A map of New London and Groton showing the placement of the forts in relation to the town. On September 6, 1781, under the command of Brigadier General Benedict Arnold, British forces landed on both shores of the Thames River, captured both forts and burned New London. *Fairfield Museum and History Center.*

except for an earthworks and a single cannon—for sustained defense. The British were, so far, ignorant of this fact and didn't dare approach. *Defence* made it up the river within range of Fort Trumbull's guns. The frigates broke away and dropped anchor off Goshen Reef, south of Alewife Cove. *Defence* was safe for now. But the geography ultimately lay in the Royal Navy's favor. Those two frigates, HMS *Amazon* and HMS *Niger*, were the beginnings of a blockade at the river's mouth.[78]

It had been a successful cruise. Unlike with the three Scottish transports, the men of *Defence* actually received the fruits of *John*. The accounting went like this: from the total price of the sale were deducted the costs of condemnation and libeling—filing the paperwork with the court and so forth—and also one-twentieth was taken off the top for the admiral of the Continental navy, as dictated by Congress. One-third of the remainder was then paid to Harding and the crew to be disbursed among them, amounting £716.12s.10d. The other two-thirds went to the state.[79]

But this is where Connecticut and Congress diverged. Although the original Continental system had been one-third for the captors and two-thirds for the state or the Continental government, Congress had on October 30, 1776, upped the ante for its own navy to half for the captors and half for the government on "merchantmen, transports, and store ships." This mirrored the scheme in place among privateers, which generally divided all prizes fifty-fifty between owners and crew. Congress expected and wanted both their naval ships and privateers to target merchant vessels—they were not as well defended and had valuable cargo that could be sold. They also knew it was foolish to pit themselves directly against the Royal Navy. But more so, the members of Congress knew from their previous experiences with boycotts that English merchants could be maneuvered into pressuring Parliament and the king for peace if their interests were damaged. Greater hurt could be inflicted by stabbing England through the pocketbook than through the heart; merchant outrage over American boycotts had been a primary factor in the repeal of the Stamp Act. Nonetheless, to encourage attacks on British warships and privateers, the share on them was increased from half of their value for the captors to 100 percent of the prize money.[80]

Connecticut didn't follow suit, instead paying only one-third of *John* to the crew of *Defence*. As the war progressed, this discrepancy between the two systems, of which the sailors were very aware, would become the snakebite in the heel of Connecticut's navy.

By December 1776, the leadership of *Defence* was falling apart. "Mr. Bartram is a good deale unwill," wrote Harding to Trumbull on the twelfth, "and in my opinion Not Capable to go on this Cruise for which I am Verry sorry for his illness." He was, the captain added, "a man of Curig" and asked that he keep receiving his pay. The council appears to have disagreed, instead dismissing Bartram without any mention of continuing his salary.[81]

Nine days later, Harding was complaining from his home in Norwich. "I am in a very poor State of Health at present & it is very uncertain whether I shall be able to go to sea," he wrote. "I therefore think it Highly Necessary to Send the Brigg to Sea I would Recommend Mr. Smedly to take Command of Sd Brigg."[82]

Harding had gout. As proteins and purines disintegrate in the body, uric acid is produced, which can then accumulate in the bloodstream. The body either produces too much uric acid or it fails to excrete it sufficiently through the kidneys; the malady is often associated with high-protein diets, including large quantities of red meat and shellfish. The uric acid deposits in joints, often at the base of the big toe, where the sharp crystalline structure of the acid causes inflammation and extreme pain. This is gout. The disorder was so common at the time that the eighteenth century has been called "the golden age of gout"; it tormented Benjamin Franklin, Thomas Jefferson and even George III. Purgatives and bleeding were the common remedy, as they depleted the level of uric acid in the body. It's instructive that back in June, when Harding was laid up at John Bradford's house in Boston, Harding was given an emetic and bled by the doctors and, within days, bounced out of bed to return to *Defence*.[83]

But now a fresh attack had beset him. "The Docters has packed me up perhaps I may Serve for one Cruse," wrote Harding, "if not I Desire Mr. Samuel Smedly to take the Command of the Brig Defence." As in his last epistle, Harding again recommended Smedley for the first lieutenancy, which at the moment hadn't been filled. "However hope your Honour

A portrait of Samuel Smedley in the uniform of a Continental naval captain. It is uncertain what uniform, if any, was worn by officers of the Connecticut state ships, but Smedley and others may have outfitted themselves at their own expense. *William D. Lee.*

will give Smedly orders to get Redey to proceed to Sea as fast as posable if am well a nuf to go Shall be glad to Step onbord and push to Sea."[84]

And so Smedley was promoted to first lieutenant onboard *Defence* and issued with accompanying orders "to sail on a cruise for three months, and that in case Capt. Harding is unable to sail the first lieutenant to take the command." Harding meanwhile convalesced in Norwich, tallying the brig's expenses for settlement. "I have no thoughts I shall be able to proceed to Sea I have but Little Hope of Ever getting my helth but god only nose."[85]

Samuel Smedley, age twenty-three, was captain of the Connecticut state brig *Defence*. The British would suffer for it.

Chapter 5

"Mr Smedleys Behavior"

I did myself the Honor of writing to you on the 14th instant by Mr. Lewis which I doubt not you have receiv'd by him I mentioned my hearing of the Arrival of the Bark taken by Capt Smedley."[86]

"Honord Sir, It is with the greatest pleasure I am able to inform you of the arrival of the Schooner Anna on Saturday Eveng, Captured by Capt Smedley."[87]

To Jonathan Alden, brig *Defence* at sea: "You are hereby ordered to take Command of the brig Grog and carry her into Sum Port in america."[88]

"It is with the greatest pleasure I am able to inform your Hnor of the arrival of the Snow Swift in Boston Harbor."[89]

In the spring of 1777, Samuel Eliot, Connecticut's agent in Boston, galloped up and down the Massachusetts seaboard, securing the prizes Smedley sent rolling in. He had cause for worry. In early December 1776, a large fleet of British warships and troop transports began collecting at the mouth of the Thames River, some arriving from the east, others from New York. An invasion of New London seemed imminent. Trumbull and the council ordered wheat and other stores in New London to be removed upriver to Norwich while garrisoning the town with militia. The fleet of an estimated one hundred soon moved up Narragansett Bay, to the relief of the town's anxious citizens, but the British maintained a steely grip on the eastern Sound. Some thirty vessels, including the frigate

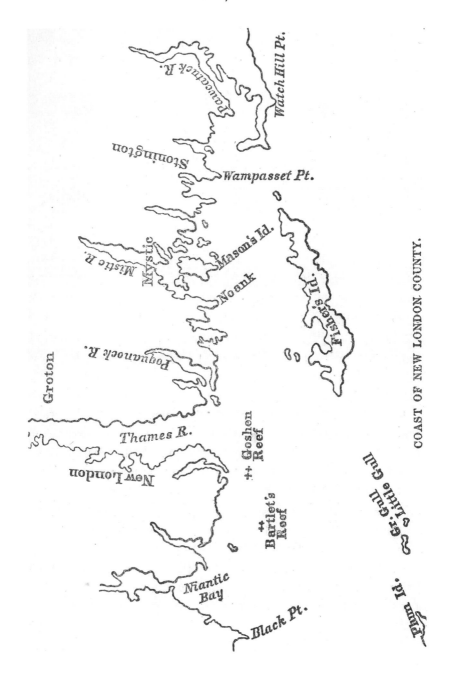

The coast of New London County. *From Frances Manwaring Caulkins's* History of New London, Connecticut.

Amazon, patrolled off New London throughout the spring and summer of 1777, seizing American ships, scouring coastal farms and Fisher's Island for livestock and food and cutting timber. "I am Informed the harbor of New London is Will Lined with Enemies Ships as it was when we Sailed by Which I found Dificult in Getting Out," wrote Smedley to the governor from New Bedford. New London was a blockaded city.[90]

This left the returning prizes susceptible to recapture. "I mentioned my hearing of the Arrival of the Bark taken by Capt Smedley at Dartmouth," wrote Eliot from New Bedford, "but my information was wrong, she put into a place call'd Woods Hole, very much expos'd to the Enemy, and on my arrival in this Place, it was the general Opinion she would be retaken." Eliot hired a boat to take him across Buzzards Bay to Woods Hole where he could secure the cargo, but before he embarked, he saw the prize enter the harbor. It mounted ten carriage guns, four swivels and, most importantly, carried two full and five half barrels of gunpowder. "As the powder is an Article in great demand, I shall order it out and shall make preparations to unload the whole Cargo as soon as possible."[91]

Within days of Eliot writing those words, thousands of miles to the south Smedley put a prize crew aboard *Grog*, a brig bound out of Glasgow loaded with beef and butter for the plantations on Antigua. Having managed to run past the British Navy in Long Island Sound, *Defence* sailed to the sixteenth latitude just outside the Lesser Antilles, where captain and crew began picking off merchant ships.[92]

Manning prizes was a tricky business. Smedley had to put *Grog* under the command of a competent bunch of sailors who weren't liable to get drunk or run off with it or wreck it. But he was reluctant to spare any of his senior officers, whom he knew better and trusted more because they were needed on *Defence*. Often the original crew was still onboard the prize, stewing below decks in irons, waiting for any opportunity to avenge themselves and retake the vessel—which sometimes happened, though it seems Smedley's custom was to take them onto *Defence*. When he arrived at New Bedford in April, he reported two hundred in his hold. To overcome the reluctance a prize crew might have in fulfilling the task, members were offered full shares not only in that prize but in any others the *Defence* might make after their departure, until the end of the cruise. "Take Good Care that there is No Plundering onboard," wrote Smedley in his orders to Midshipman Jonathan Alden, the *Grog*'s prize master; the ship's cargo had to be brought in secure if the court was to award it to *Defence*. He also explicitly directed Alden to inform Eliot and Trumbull of the capture as soon as they made port.[93]

The three other prizes Smedley took during the cruise arrived safely: the bark into New Bedford, *Anna* and *Swift* into Boston. But Smedley's faith in Alden seems to have been misplaced. "On Monday last an account was handed me of the arrival of a Prize taken by Capt Smedley in at Plymouth," wrote Eliot. He rode for Plymouth to secure the vessel where "to my very great Sorrow I found her run on Shore so high up as it would be impossible to gett her off without unloading, as it was my Duty I engage'd a sloop to lay along side and take as much of her Cargo out as will lighten and gett her off the Barr. The Sloop is to proceed to Boston the remainder is to be kept on board untill further orders." Headaches, always headaches.[94]

Connecticut had bought the original brig "for the use of this Colony, to be fitted and improved as an armed vessel for the defence thereof," but now the mission had changed. *Defence* was not defending the New England seacoast or the towns along Long Island Sound or anything else; it was striking out—and not at ships of war but rather at merchant vessels. The prize money of the three Scottish transports captured in June 1776 had flowed to the naval agent John Bradford, where it evaporated, offsetting debts incurred by other vessels and other ventures. In contrast, the state had received its two-thirds and the men their shares from *John* and its cargo. At every meeting of Trumbull and his Council of Safety, orders were issued and expenses generated, backed only by IOUs and property tax increases to be paid in the future. But the guns and powder of merchant ships could be used for the state's military commitments, while the vessels and their cargoes could be sold at auction for hard money. Attacking the Royal Navy simply didn't pay for the state or the officers and crew of *Defence*—hitting British commerce did.[95]

Back in January, Trumbull and the council had resolved "that discretionary orders be given to the commander of the *Defence* to join with other privateers if thought best in an expedition against the vessells and wood-cutters at Shelter Island." Smedley decided against this course, probably because it wasn't ambitious enough. Shelter Island is a small isle located between Long Island's eastern forks. It was thickly wooded and sparsely populated at the time—at most twenty-seven households, their slaves and a small population of Native Americans—and dedicated to the Patriot cause. The British maintained a strong presence in Gardiners Bay and sometimes came ashore on Shelter Island to abuse and thieve from the residents. There was also a British garrison at Sag Harbor, directly opposite the island on the South Fork. The expedition mentioned by the council did come to pass: in May 1777, thirteen whaleboats sailed from Guilford, Connecticut, stayed overnight in Peconic Bay and, early the next morning, executed a lightning raid against the garrison, destroying twelve British vessels and returning to Connecticut with ninety prisoners and stores without a single loss. That was all well and good for a flotilla of whaleboats but peanuts for *Defence*.[96]

Trumbull and his council were more than satisfied with Smedley's decision. In two months' time, the state suddenly had four vessels and their cargoes in hand, with no other claimants to bicker with. By summer, the legalities were resolved and the assets liquidated. The flour and butter onboard *Anna* and *Swift* were sold in Boston, with the ships themselves advertised to the Board of War should they want to purchase them for the navy. The *Grog* run aground was easy to deal with: Eliot simply sold the beef, pork and butter still aboard to the locals in Plymouth. And clearly Trumbull wanted Smedley to keep doing what he did; a week after *Defence* arrived back in port, he and the council permanently appointed Smedley as the brig's captain.[97]

First order of business: "I would Recommend to your honour," wrote Smedley, "by all means Lengthen the brig and put a quarter deck on her that She may be in a better to Fight Which now She is not & most the uncomfortable Vessel that ever I was in." Adding length would increase living room below decks—it must have been cramped quarters with a crew of at least one hundred men, plus prisoners and stores—while a quarter deck would provide some advantage of height for mounting swivel guns. He suggested the work could be done in Boston in a short time, although he was ready to sail if the governor disagreed.[98]

It was an expensive proposal. It was one thing to spend money fitting the brig for a voyage, but it was another to commit slim resources to renovate a vessel that otherwise had proven capable of doing its job. Trumbull mulled it over. In the meantime, the council voted "to give liberty to Capt. Smedley to consort with the privateer belonging to Thos. Mumford, Esqr, and others, in a cruise, or not as he pleases."[99]

Whether Smedley took that cruise is uncertain; he and the *Defence* fade from view for much of the summer of 1777, reappearing in August at Boston. There are no reports of any prizes. The fact is that he may not have been able to retain enough crew to go anywhere. Smedley complained to Trumbull that back in February, while *Defence* waited in New London for the British to clear, a number of sailors deserted; meanwhile, every idle day brought him closer to March 1, which was when many of the men's terms expired. So Smedley threw caution to the winds because "their [*sic*] was no chance for to make a Cruise unless we put to Sea with what we had." Now that they were back in port, the captain expected the rest to leave as well.[100]

Smedley was an aggressive recruiter. William Coit, captain of the state's new twenty-gun *Oliver Cromwell*, fresh off the ways at Saybrook, complained of his tactics. Like Smedley, in February 1777, Coit was attempting to fill billets so he could raise anchor but was stymied by his fellows-in-arms. "The Engaging of men if they were not taken from me by every species of designing men," Coit groused to Trumbull, "who with large promises entice them away would be very easy to engage. Mr Elderkin will inform you of Mr Smedleys behavior!"[101]

By late August, Trumbull was amenable to Smedley's plan and ordered Eliot to see it through. "I think it is expedient to have the Brig Defence lengthened, & to give her a Quarter Deck & Sides, & other repairs to fit her for Sea, have given orders to Capt. Smedley for that purpose I wish you to give him every assistance in your power." Eliot obeyed, reporting the next month that the *Defence* "is now on the ways and divided—Capt. Smedley has given her Eighteen feet in length—which will add fourteen Inches to her beam, all who have Seen her give it as their opinion, she will make a compleat Vessel." The council also ordered that a third mast be added, transforming *Defence* from a brig to a proper ship, and for it to be rigged accordingly. Eliot prudently recycled the "Cables & Cordage" from the *Honor*, a prize brought in by *Oliver Cromwell*, for *Defence*'s improvement. But it was not a speedy process. The refurbishment stretched into December as Eliot paid for deck nails, sheathing nails, lead, cordage, turpentine and, of course, gallons upon gallons of rum for the workers. By the end of the year, the bill tallied over £704.[102]

A scale model of the ship *Defence* by William D. Lee. *Fairfield Museum and History Center.*

Even that wasn't enough. "Your Excellency cannot think how exceeding expensive ships are fitted out at this Day," wrote Smedley to Trumbull in February 1778. The renovation was complete; the ship had victuals except "bread and flour and small stores," and a crew of one hundred were aboard and ready to sail. But Smedley needed more money. He had "taken unweared Pain" to recruit men in Falmouth, on the Cape, the Vineyard and elsewhere, all of which was expensive. In Boston, he had recruited only three or four men; there were fourteen other armed vessels in the harbor with which to compete. Smedley had spent the money Trumbull had sent for provisioning to recruit so far afield; now he needed more to pay the back wages due the men. "Your Excellency Doubtless knows the Expences She is attended with therefore my Reasons for Troubling your Excellency at this time Is to beg the Authority to Supply our agent with Cash sufficient to send us to sea Immediately…I hope soon to Pay the state threefold for all her Expenses."[103]

It came back to the division of prizes. Earlier that year, in May, just after *Defence* had returned to port behind *Anna*, *Grog* and the rest, Eliot wrote to Trumbull, begging direction on how the prizes should be divided. The crewmen were very upset to learn they were only entitled to one-third of each and angrily descended upon Eliot. "Some brot Copys of the Shipping papers, which mentions 'they were on the Same footing as the Continental Navy'"—meaning they expected half of the prizes, not one-third. These were the "large promises" Coit complained of earlier. "I did all in my power to make Officers and privates easy," wrote Eliot, even going so far as to distribute £1,200 among them to cool their tempers. "It was the most weighty argument I could make use off."[104]

Even before the cruise, the division issue had impeded Smedley. In February, just as *Defence* was ready to leave New London, Smedley was delayed when Henry Billings, the man he thought was going to serve as a lieutenant for the cruise, declined the commission. Billings sent the paper back to Trumbull with apologies, explaining that he couldn't sail with *Defence* "for no other Reason than that I am offered the Command of a Burmudian Built Sloop fixing out as a Privateer—And I think to do Justice to myself & family I must except of the offer." Privateers, again unlike the state naval system, earned half of prizes, and Billings had mouths to feed. So instead of sailing, *Defence* was again forced to lay idle while Smedley scrambled to find a replacement.[105]

Trumbull, not unaware of the difficulty, agreed on a temporary compromise. So, "in order to proceed on their respective cruises," the governor and the council in December 1777 made a one-time exception for *Defence* and *Oliver Cromwell*, resolving that "officers, seamen and marines…shall be entitled to a division of one half of all their captures, whether ships of war, armed or other vessels…and the other half to be and belong to this State." This, it was believed, would encourage recruitment and allow the two ships to finally sail.[106]

Now came Smedley's request for more money to pay the crew's wages. Trumbull and the council acquiesced but signaled that their patience was dwindling. They issued £4,000 to Eliot "for the purpose of fitting out (as soon as possible) the ship *Defence* and the ship *Oliver Cromwell*." The funds were accompanied by sailing orders for both ships. Smedley badly needed to get to sea and make some money.[107]

Chapter 6

"A WARM
COMBAT INSUED"

O n My First Weighing Anchor in Boston Harbour I Found A Man on Board Broke out With the Small-Pox," wrote Smedley to Trumbull while at sea. After they cleared the harbor, the captain sent the man back on the pilot's boat to prevent an outbreak. "But to my Sorrow It had not the Desired Affect, for on the 13th Day from Boston I had Six Broke out With the Same Disorder, two of Which is Since Dead."[108]

By that point, *Defence* was well underway, and it wasn't a matter of putting the six afflicted men on a boat and sending them into port. Smedley held a council with his officers. They discovered, when tallying up the crew, that "Upwards of Fifty on Board" had never had smallpox or been inoculated against it. That meant half or nearly half of the crew was susceptible. Smedley was facing an epidemic throughout his little island of wood and canvas.[109]

He didn't have many options. He could have sailed back to Boston or some other port and tried to dump the men, but more than likely the harbor master would have quarantined the ship, leaving them no better than before. He could have isolated the sick men somehow, hoped it didn't spread and let the chips fall where they may. Or if he was a monster, he could have abandoned the six to their fate on some deserted shore.

Smedley didn't do any of these. Instead, he inoculated the fifty healthy men at sea.

Variola major, or smallpox, is a highly infectious virus. It enters into the respiratory system through droplets expelled from the nose and mouth or transmitted from the hand to the face. Smallpox can also survive without a host for weeks, lurking in bedding or linens. It has an incubation stage of about two weeks, during which it spreads through the lymph nodes. The first visible symptoms include high fever and aching limbs, head and back. Two to four days later a rash appears, forming pustules that fill with liquid, rupture and weep. In cases where the pustules overlap, called confluent smallpox, the victim has at least a 60 percent chance of dying. After eight or ten days of this, scabs form over the sores, or the victim simply dies. At about three weeks, the fever ebbs and the scabs begin to shed, often leaving deep scarring and sometimes blindness in one or both eyes.[110]

Smallpox had plagued mankind since the days of Pharaonic Egypt, and one eighteenth-century estimate holds that fifteen million died of it every twenty-five years, as an epidemic swept through, killed and allowed a fresh unexposed population to grow up, only to be cut down again. This number is now believed to have been modest. Survivors of smallpox gain a lifelong immunity to it, which led to the process of inoculation, in which material from a smallpox pustule was inserted into an incision made in the skin of a healthy person. Though the person develops smallpox from the live virus (vaccination, which uses weakened or dead virus, wasn't established until 1796 by Edward Jenner), the symptoms are not as intense, and the mortality rate is much lower (as small as 2 percent). The reason for this is not understood even today. Inoculation was practiced widely outside of Europe but not in Britain until 1721, when the wife of the ambassador to the Ottoman Empire returned home and popularized it. From there, the practice spread to the colonies.[111]

This wasn't the first time Smedley was exposed to smallpox. Back in 1776, after the battle with three Scottish ships, Harding quickly departed Boston because of an outbreak; when he returned to Connecticut in July, the captain and the council discussed what to do "about the men who are probably infected with the small pox." Smedley doesn't seem to have contracted it then nor did he seem concerned about his personal risk at sea in 1778; either he had it previously, perhaps as a child, or he had already been inoculated.[112]

The dispatch with which Smedley decided to inoculate his sailors suggests he had been through it and knew what the men could expect. But if so, then where had he been inoculated and when? Inoculation was not looked upon fondly in New England. People feared that an inoculated person could infect others beyond the hospital, leading to an outbreak. Because unregulated inoculation "may create great disorders and disquietudes, much endanger the people, and frustrate the good end of the law," Connecticut in 1760 banned inoculation unless both doctor and patient first obtained permission from the selectmen of the town in which the inoculation took place. The selectmen were also directed to assign houses for the procedure, approve nurses and create a host of safeguards. One history of Fairfield notes that, in 1756, the town granted permission to Gideon Wells (the same doctor with whom Smedley quarreled onboard *Defence*) to establish a hospital to inoculate against smallpox. For a seaport like Fairfield, this made sense; with sailors frequently traveling to Boston, New York and the West Indies, risk of contamination was great not just for them but for everybody in town. Perhaps Smedley had been inoculated as a child; his father could afford the high cost of the procedure. Or perhaps he had been inoculated more recently. When General Washington informed Governor Trumbull that he intended to inoculate troops in the Continental army, the council abandoned its previous reservations and exclaimed that it had "no objection to so salutary a measure, upon which depends not only the lives of all the men who have not had the small pox but also the health of the whole army." Hospitals were established throughout the state to inoculate new soldiers; presumably members of the state navy could volunteer for it, too. After the war, Fairfield grew so comfortable with the procedure that residents began inoculating themselves without doctors.[113]

Fortunately, *Defence* didn't sail alone. The *Oliver Cromwell* accompanied them on the cruise, captained by Timothy Parker. The brand-new ship had originally been commanded by William Coit, but after months of sitting idle in New London Harbor while complaining he couldn't recruit enough crew—and accumulating questions about his bookkeeping of ship's funds—Coit was dismissed in April 1777 and replaced by a recuperated Seth Harding. For the rest of 1777, *Oliver Cromwell* sailed under Harding, bringing in two prizes, *Honor* and *Weymouth*. By the end

The HMS *Rose* in Black Rock Harbor as part of the 1989 commemoration of the burning of Fairfield. The *Rose* is a recreation of an eighteenth-century Royal Navy frigate. At twenty guns, she is comparable in size and rigging to *Oliver Cromwell*. *Fairfield Museum and History Center.*

of the year, Harding's illness overcame him again. As with *Defence*, his first lieutenant replaced him as captain: Timothy Parker, a Cape Cod transplant to Norwich just like Harding.[114]

Smedley and Parker got along well. "Ever Since our Acquaintance," wrote Smedley, "there has been the Greatest Union Between Us & has in My Distressful situation Given me much Asistance." Parker agreed: "There is a great harmony Subsisting Between us and I think we have been mutually Serviceable to Each other."[115]

The two ships sailed south toward the West Indies. Again, though these were the largest vessels of Connecticut's fleet, there was no thought of taking on the Royal Navy in Long Island Sound or freeing New London from its blockade. Merchant ships, even letters of marque, were comparatively easy to take and much more lucrative for state and sailor alike.

On April 10, 1778, a sail was spotted, and by nightfall, the vessel was "brought to." Smedley hailed her, but the reply came in French, which

Smedley didn't speak. As luck would have it, one of his crewmembers did and translated. Relations were cordial between Americans and Frenchmen; the two nations had signed the Treaty of Alliance in February, which precipitated England to declare war on France the following month. The United States and France were now in this together. And so, in esprit de corps, the French captain was invited onboard *Defence* for supper.[116]

The French captain had news for Smedley. Earlier that very day, the French ship had parted with two English ships out of Bristol, one mounting eighteen guns, the other twenty, "deep loaded" and bound for Jamaica. (It's odd the Britishers didn't attack the French ship, but perhaps their captains were ignorant of the recent state of war between the two countries.) Smedley thanked the French captain and returned him to his ship. *Defence* and *Oliver Cromwell* immediately bent all sail "on the Course We thought Best to Fall in with them."[117]

Smedley ordered the boatswain to pipe all hands on deck. There he related the information told to him by the French captain and asked his crew if they were prepared to give chase and fight for the prizes. The men shouted an affirmative. They sat up all night making bandages and scraping lint "so that we might be prepared to dress our wounds, as we expected to have a hard time of it."[118]

At daybreak the following morning, they spotted two sails to the southeast about six miles off. The chase lasted all day. By nine at night, they had caught up to *Cyrus* and *Admiral Keppel*. French colors flew from the Britishers' sheets, but once the Connecticut ships were within a mile and a half, the Union Jack replaced them. "We soon was A Long Side," Smedley wrote, "& A Warm Combat Insued Which Lasted for three Glasses" (a "glass" was a turning of the hourglass used to measure time onboard ship, a half-hour with every turn). *Cyrus*'s poor marksmanship meant *Defence* didn't come off too badly. "The Hole Rigging of my Ship was Much Damaged," wrote Smedley in a letter to Trumbull via the prize master put aboard *Cyrus* and sent into Boston. "We have but two Men Wounded Which [I] am in Hopes will do well." The victory is all the more impressive considering half the crew was sick with smallpox, "taken Down at A Time when they were most Wanted."[119]

It was left to Captain Parker and the crew of *Oliver Cromwell* to subdue *Admiral Keppel*, which "made a verry warlike appearance and was the best mand Ship by some considerable odds," in Parker's words. *Oliver Cromwell* set in pursuit, firing the bow gun and *Admiral Keppel* replying with her chase guns. Volleys of grape and round shot followed. Parker refused to answer, ordering his men "not to fire till we Can See the white of their Eyes." Closer and closer they raced. *Admiral Keppel* fired another broadside, and this time *Oliver Cromwell* answered. "She gave me a warm reception for about three glasses when she thought proper to Strike," wrote Parker.[120]

Oliver Cromwell suffered much worse casualties than *Defence*. "I unfortunately had one man killed outright"; the captain of marines was mortally injured, dying three days after the battle; "two others with their thighs broke which I fear will not Recover"; and three more wounded through the arm, leg and shoulder. But Parker noted, "the Courage and Bravery of my raw undisciplined men cannot fail of Doing honour to their Country."[121]

The Connecticut ships spent a few days taking prisoners out the prizes and making repairs. Though *Defence* had fared well in the battle, the ship was leaky and had been since leaving Boston, a difficulty exacerbated by the fact that one of the two men who had died of smallpox was the chief carpenter. *Oliver Cromwell*, again had taken the greater damage in the battle, "had four shot Between wind and water," shrouds and ropes cut in two, the "Sails a little tatered." Both vessels were well enough to spend another month prowling. They lost sight of the prizes on the northern horizon, en route to Boston, on April 21. In early May, they chased a sail that turned out to be another French ship; they put six of their prisoners onboard and sent her away. A few days later, the two were chased by a twenty-eight-gun British frigate. They outran it. Finally, requiring more substantial repairs and supplies, *Defence* and *Oliver Cromwell* turned north for Charleston, South Carolina, arriving "over the Bar" and into the harbor on May 30.[122]

Parker had another reason for visiting Charleston. Earlier, Joseph Trumbull—son of the governor, former commissary general and now appointed business agent for the state—had arranged for *Oliver Cromwell* to transport a cargo of indigo from Charleston to Nantes, France, where it would be sold. Connecticut, like its twelve fellows, badly needed hard currency. The states spent thousands on the war effort every day but had no means beyond taxes to pay for it, which seemed all the more dubious considering so many were occupied in the unprofitable business of fighting the British. Rose and Torrans, the state's agents in Charleston, remarked that although quantities of commodities like rice were less than before, they still sold for the same price as prior to the war, "the reason of this is the want of shipping to carry it off." Without the means to transport to market, commodity prices were depressed even though supplies were diminished. And so Connecticut's warships took a further step away from their original mission to become merchant vessels. Upon its arrival, the mighty twenty-gun *Oliver Cromwell* delivered a load of linen to Rose and Torrans for sale in Charleston.[123]

Smedley, meanwhile, and the crew of *Defence* were not allowed to enter the city due to the smallpox. "Although they have been free from it for near a month, She is obliged to perform quarantine," wrote the agents. "There is no time fixed but hope in 8 or 10 days that she will be allowed to come up to Town." The sailors scraped the barnacles off as best they could—"the Ship being so very foul"—and waited for clearance, "not with standing the Repeated Promises I had of being Permitted Every Week." They waited and waited. Permission didn't come.[124]

So Smedley went hunting.

"On receiving intelligence of several of the Enemys privateers being on our coast & annoying our trade with impunity," wrote Rose and Torrans to Joseph Trumbull, "Capt Smedley (notwithstanding he was at the time performing quarantine for the smallpox) on an application from His Excellency our President, fitted out the Defence immediately." The English privateers had been a festering thorn in Charleston's side, reportedly taking thirty-four Patriot vessels. Members of South Carolina's own navy, including captains Robeson and McQueen and even its commodore, Alexander Gillon, leapt to join the expedition. On June 19, *Defence* "sailed over our Bar in quest of them," accompanied by a French sloop named *Volant*, captained by Oliver Daniel.[125]

Smedley appointed lookouts on the fore- and mainmasts. Less than an hour after crossing the sandbar, two sails were spotted. The Charleston volunteers "said they were the two sloops that had been cruising, and told captain Smedly he would have his belly full of them."[126]

Smedley ordered the cannons housed, the port holes shuttered, for the bulk of the men to hide themselves—just enough hands to work the ship. *Defence* made herself appear like a simple merchant marine.

Soon one of the English privateers came within distance.

"Ahoy! the ship ahoy! from whence came you?"

Smedley put the speaking trumpet to his mouth. "From South Carolina," he answered.

"Where are you bound?"

"Alongside you, you rascals!" Smedley gave the order: "Out guns, boys!"

The ports flew open, and the sixteen six-pounders slid into view. *Defence*'s marines jumped on deck, cutlasses waving, throats screaming. Gunners manned the swivels.

"Haul down your colours, or I will sink you instantly," ordered Smedley. "Round too, and come under my stern."

The English privateer obliged.[127]

The second ship ran, but *Defence* caught up and likewise took it without a shot. The two prizes were the *Governor Tonyn's Revenge*, twelve carriage guns and seventy-two men, and *Ranger*, eight guns, thirty-five men, both privateers out of St. Augustine. There was a third—*Active* from Liverpool, twelve guns, fifty-seven men—that "would have been likewise taken, but took advantage of the near approach of night and thick weather, and made off," while Smedley was securing prisoners from the others.[128]

Defence and *Volant*, their two prizes accompanying them, returned to a hero's welcome in Charleston. "We were saluted from Fort Sullivan and Fort Johnson," one crewmember recalled, "and colours were hoisted from every gentleman's house, who was not a tory." There was no longer a question of quarantine. "Capt Smedley has acquired great reputation on this occasion & has done an official service to the commercial interest of this state," wrote Rose & Torrans.[129]

For their part, the agents claimed half of each prize in *Defence*'s name, "which will we hope go a great way towards paying the expenses & outfit of the *Oliver Cromwell* & *Defence*." The prizes sold for "upwards of £80,000" and were split three ways between *Volant*, *Defence* and South Carolina.[130]

Smedley and the crew received their prize money, though indirectly. Trumbull and the council ordered Eliot in Boston to pay the men their shares "for the prizes sent into Carolina," drawing on funds either forwarded to him by the state or derived from the sale of other prizes (most likely from *Cyrus*, which, along with *Admiral Keppel*, had safely arrived into Boston). Rose and Torrans never sent the actual prize money from *Governor Tonyn's Revenge* or *Ranger* to Connecticut; on the contrary, the state owed them. While in Charleston, *Defence* and *Oliver Cromwell* together racked up over £56,511 worth of expenses, "equal to 34,801 Dollars which is placed to yours & the Debt of the States," wrote Rose and Torrans to Joseph Trumbull. The prize money covered the bulk of it but still left Rose and Torrans holding the balance. The agents wrote long letters to Trumbull, painting rosy portraits of privateer booty just beyond Charleston—"its impossible for Privateers to miss making there fortune as they have this Port so near to them, to send their prises to"— in an attempt to generate more prize revenue and therefore pay off the debt, but their letters went unanswered, in large part because they were corresponding with a dead man: Joseph Trumbull had died of illness in July. Rose and Torrans continued to dig a deeper hole for themselves until well into 1779, drawing on Connecticut's credit for other state officials and captains who passed through before finally giving up. Their last letter to the deceased Trumbull ends: "I hope in case of futer transactions, that you will contrive to place funds in our hands."[131]

With repairs made and the accounts signed, *Oliver Cromwell* and *Defence* parted ways. Parker and the *Oliver Cromwell*, its hold full of indigo, lay in the harbor for weeks. "I have had great Trouble with my people here on Account of the Ships going to France—many of them have Deserted the Ship, which has caused great Delay and Incured great Expence," Parker wrote. Finally they sailed in late July. They chased some sails between the Bahamas and Florida, hoping to catch prizes from the Jamaica Fleet. Then, on August 24, a hurricane slammed into the ship off the Bahama Banks. The crew cut away all her masts, the anchor, too, and managed to ride it out. Jury rigged, they finally limped into New London in early September, their cargo of France-bound indigo still below decks.[132]

Defence appears to have sailed straight back to Boston without taking any prizes, though they had one fortuitous encounter. A large schooner was brought about and found to be loaded with passengers: Tories escaping to British-held St. Augustine. Smedley allowed them passage. First, though, he confiscated all of their money.[133]

By mid-September 1778, Smedley was back in Fairfield attempting to recruit for another voyage. But the same old obstruction again confounded him: prize division. The fifty-fifty scheme under which *Defence* and *Oliver Cromwell* sailed south to Charleston had been for that cruise only. Now, the state ships were once again on the one-third/two-thirds formula. They couldn't compete with either the Continental navy or privateers. In Fairfield, Smedley only found two men willing to sign aboard *Defence*. "The Last Cruize, I had from this, & the neighboring Towns near one half of my Crew, the greater part of which are now in the Continental and other state service, owing to the Singular Laws of this state," wrote Smedley to Trumbull. The governor apparently agreed with Smedley, but his Council of Safety did not—doing so meant surrendering money the state desperately needed. But there wouldn't be any prize money to begin with if *Defence* and the other state ships didn't have enough men to sail them out of the harbor. If Connecticut adopted the Continental model, Smedley wrote, "I can assure them it would be the only means of upholding our Navy."[134]

Parker, having sent officers to enlist for *Oliver Cromwell* in both New London and Norwich, had the same gripe. Between the two ports, Parker could find only seven men willing to join. As the *Oliver Cromwell* was fitted and repaired, he tried to chat up the workers but to no result. "Several that have been at work on board with Intention to go in the Ship finding her going on the old plan, have since left her and gone to the Confederacy," he wrote. *Confederacy* was a new Continental frigate, thirty-two guns, built upriver from New London and captained by Seth Harding who had once again recovered, this time well enough to join the Continental navy. With Harding's successful track record and the promise of a bigger piece of a prize, the state ships couldn't compete for recruits. "Mr Angel," wrote Parker, referring to Smedley's first mate, "tells me the case is quite Similar with the *Defence*." Like Smedley, Parker wanted Connecticut to put them on an equal footing with Continental vessels. Parker, Angel and Parker's first lieutenant, John Chapman, all signed the letter, opining, "Unless that is the case [the state ships] cannot be got to Sea without great Delay and Extraordinary Expence if at all."[135]

By January 1779, *Defence* was still yawing at anchor in Black Rock Harbor. Crew wasn't the only thing in short supply—so was the bread to feed them. Smedley rode the countryside searching for wheat but doubted he could acquire enough, complaining that "there's no more

The Continental frigate *Confederacy*, armed with twenty-eight twelve-pound and eight six-pound cannons. Launched in November 1778, she was commanded by Seth Harding. *Confederacy* was captured by the British in 1781. *Navy Art Gallery, U.S. Navy.*

Dependence Upon A Farmer at this day than Upon the Divel, nay I think he would be Ashamed to behave in the Manner they do." Thomas Cable, a local miller and baker, also scoured the countryside for wheat to bake into ship's bread for *Defence*. The wheat existed, but the problem lay in the near collapse of the economy. Cable wrote to Nathaniel Shaw, volunteering his services "if I could Purchase the Wheat Which wood be Defecult to Do for money." Continental dollars were worthless, and in wartime, even British pound sterling and Spanish dollars were unwanted. "If You wood Advance Some Westinde goods and Perhaps Some Other Articles Which you have on hand," wrote Cable, he could barter them "for as much Wheat as I Cold Bake Sir."[136]

For five months, both state ships were idle. The general assembly became so frustrated that they appointed a commission to discover the causes why. The committee's answer quickly returned—"that tis extreamly difficult to procure Men to enter on board"—accompanied with its recommendation: "that the same Dividend of the prizes which the Ships shall take, be made to the Crews which has been usually made on board private Ships of Warr," half for the captors, half for the state.

The assembly had none of the reservations of the Council of Safety; they immediately agreed to the committee's plan, both houses voting that *Defence* and *Oliver Cromwell* operate on the fifty-fifty scheme.[137]

It was too little, too late. *Defence* returned to New London in February. The chances there for recruiting were just as grim as in Fairfield, but Smedley and Parker appear to have hammered out an interim solution with Trumbull and the council. A detachment of Continental troops originally from Connecticut were stationed at the forts surrounding New London. The two captains were permitted to man their vessels from the detachment. However, there would be no voyages to the West Indies to strike at merchant marines; instead, *Defence* and *Oliver Cromwell* were ordered "to go on an expedition in the Sound against the enemy in company with the continental ships and troops." As reward and enticement for those Continental troops who manned the state ships, "the shares of plunder &c. shall be as the other ships"; in other words, division of prizes would be on the Continental system.[138]

The council may have imagined that by keeping in proximity to New London, Smedley and Parker could have maintained recruitment in town while working to some purpose in the Sound. As it turns out, the arrangement, though novel, didn't last.

"I never Emplored my pen in writing more Disagreeable News than at this time," wrote Smedley to Governor Trumbull on March 12, 1779. Acting on orders from Harding aboard the *Confederacy*, "whose command I considered my Self under," *Defence* went into the Sound to report on the movements of the British ships. On their return into port—some accounts said they were pursued by Britishers, though Smedley never mentioned this—*Defence* "struck on Goshen Reef where she soon over set & bilged." Four or five men were flung into the water and drowned. The shoals ripped open *Defence*'s hull. She was breaking apart.[139]

Smedley ordered one of the detachment officers to take the ship's boat, find Nathaniel Shaw in town and have him send lighters to the wreck. The lighters soon arrived, "& after about thirty hours Fatigued up to our Middels in water we secured all our Guns Riging warlike stores Sails Provisions & every thing of any Value above water." These items went aboard the lighters and floated safely into New London.[140]

The ship *Defence*, meanwhile, dissolved in the waves. "The wind has Since been so high that no Vessell Could go along Side Since although we have made Several Tryalls," wrote Nathaniel Shaw to Trumbull. But it may not have mattered, even if they could have salvaged the ship. "Such Distres'd times for bread I never knew before," he wrote, and "Men is very Scarse." If only Connecticut had adopted the Continental system sooner, then perhaps its ships would have never struggled to recruit crew. If only Smedley had the men, *Defence* could have raided the West Indies indefinitely, sending back rich prizes. If only *Defence* had voyaged to the West Indies instead, it would have never wrecked outside New London. If only.[141]

Chapter 7
"The Flames Have Now Preceded Your Flag"

The sinking vexed and shamed Smedley. He blamed the ship's pilot, "whose knowledge in Pilotage I had Reason to Believe was good but to my Sorrow found he knew not what he Pretended." Fearful that "I should have the censure of the Publick," he asked Trumbull for an immediate court of inquiry. It was granted.[142]

No record exists of the proceedings, no stenographer's notes, when the court sat at the tavern of Nathan Douglas on March 17, 1779. We only know the verdict. We also have the bar tab. It included six bottles of wine, eighteen bowls of punch and dinner. For six men.[143]

Smedley, of course, was one of the six, but there's scant mention of who the other five were. A tribunal likely presided as it had in Smedley's dispute with Gideon Wells in July 1776. Timothy Parker signed the innkeeper's bill, so he was there. Seth Harding and Nathaniel Shaw, both of whom were in New London at the time, were probably also present. The remaining two men may have been witnesses, perhaps James Angel, Smedley's first lieutenant, and Captain Lloyd, the Continental officer whom Smedley dispatched to bring the lighters.

Smedley could have hardly expected a bad outcome among such friends and colleagues. He was exonerated. The result pleased him so much that he requested that Trumbull publish the findings, publicly absolving him of any wrongdoing.[144]

The governor and his council likewise considered Smedley blameless. In June, they offered him a fresh commission to captain the sloop *Guilford*. This had previously been the English privateer *Mars*, eight guns. In early February, *Mars* captured an American sloop and brought its crew onboard as prisoners. The sloop was sent into New York. But later that month, the sloop's captain, Giles Sage, and his men broke free, overpowered *Mars*'s sailors and beached her in the town of Guilford. The sloop was renamed and entered into the state service.[145]

Smedley declined the commission. Having retired to Fairfield, he was too preoccupied with events there to think of leaving.

The enmity between Patriot Connecticut and Tory Long Island had erupted into a war in itself. The previous fall, the assembly had moved an entire regiment into coastal southwestern Connecticut to defend "against the incursions and depredations of the enemy by sea and land." Whaleboat raids on both sides had become common occurrences. Now, on July 2, 1779, Samuel Squire, Jonathan Sturges and Thaddeus Burr—the patriarchs of Fairfield—wrote to Trumbull with distressing news. Some two hundred Tories had gathered a fleet at Lloyd Neck, on Long Island opposite Norwalk, "to harrass and distress our Coasts." The flotilla consisted of two topsail schooners and four sloops with twenty

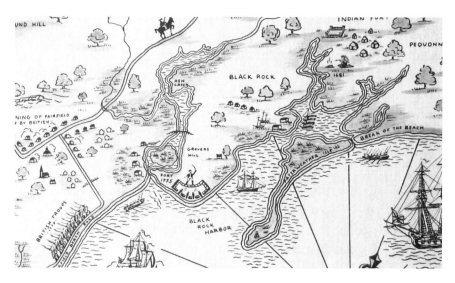

A modern map of Fairfield during the years of the American Revolution. William D. Lee. *Fairfield Museum and History Center.*

cannons between them. On June 29 or 30, they set sail, crossed the Sound and attempted to come ashore, but Stephen St. John, colonel of the company at Norwalk, "put himself in such a position as prevented their Landing."[146]

Frustrated, the fleet moved farther east along the coast to Compo Beach (then part of western Fairfield but now in Westport), where the British had landed in 1777 and marched north to the Battle of Ridgefield. Patrols there also prevented them from landing. The fleet again moved eastward.

This time the Tories came to the mouth of the Mill River. This is the same river that had to be forded several miles north of town, as it was too deep and wide to be safely crossed farther south. The Fairfield militia watched and waited. "As it was very uncertain whether thy wo'd attempt to land on the East or West side of the Bay," wrote Squire and the others, they decided to stay on the east bank rather than send others across by boat or by running up and across the ford. The force "planted ourselves in Number about 70 Men with the Field Piece behind the banks on the shore, were we supposed they wo'd land."[147]

The Loyalists approached the western shore instead. "Under cover of a very heavy firing from the Fleet," a group of Tories landed and set fire to three houses and their barns. The residents rallied and counterattacked so "that they were not onshore more than 15 minutes." The locals extinguished most of the fires, though one house and two barns were lost.[148]

Reembarked, the Loyalists made for the eastern side of the river, where the militia had dug in. "As soon as they came within point blank shoot of the Field Piece they hove too, and prepared for Action." There was no attempt at landing—the Tories were about to unleash their twenty guns on the men. The Fairfielders only had the single carriage cannon, probably a six-pounder.

"Capt Smedley, Lieut Sturgis and a Mr. Hazzard had the principle management of the piece. They fired with deliberation and good Judgement and hulled them five or six times out of eight or nine shoot." Smedley must have gained some personal experience with cannons aboard *Defence*: he batted an average of .555 to .75. "After returning us five or six shoot, we obliged them to sheer of and make the best of their way from us," wrote Squire.[149]

The Tory flotilla floated out of reach of the cannon until sundown. This allowed every able-bodied man in town to gather on the beach, where the guards were doubled for twelve miles along the shore. Seeing their advantage of surprise lost—and undoubtedly nursing some wounds—the Loyalists sailed off into the Sound, presumably for Lloyd Neck—but for how long? Squire, Sturges and Burr asked the governor to order a galley and the *Guilford*, then at New Haven, to cruise off Fairfield and Norwalk to intercept another attack. "If she is not man'd there are Volunteers enough this way."[150]

Trumbull and his council could not fulfill the request—much greater events were in motion. The Tory flotilla was no random strike by malcontents but rather part of a larger scheme.

The letter by the three men was written on Friday, July 2. On the following Sunday, the Fourth of July, under the command of Commodore Sir George Collier, two British men-of-war, *Camilla* and *Scorpion*, plus forty-eight galleys, tenders and transports sailed from Whitestone in modern-day Queens. Together they carried upward of 2,600 British troops, Hessian mercenaries and Loyalist volunteers. They cruised east through Long Island Sound, coming to anchor at New Haven. The next morning, as the town planned to celebrate the anniversary of the signing of the Declaration of Independence (the Fourth fell on the Sabbath and postponed the festivities), the troops landed in West Haven. Though harassed by shot and cannon fire from a mix of militia, townspeople and Yale students—resulting in 9 British dead, 41 wounded and 25 missing—the infantry marched into New Haven and seized the town. A promise of leniency was given to those inhabitants who did not resist the invasion. Nevertheless, "buildings were forcibly entered; articles of value, as silver plate, watches, buckles, clothing, money and the like, were taken often in a brutal manner; beds were cut to pieces or otherwise destroyed if not carried off; provisions were used or wasted; furniture was demolished; doors and windows were dashed in."[151]

The plunder continued through the night, with Patriot townspeople either fleeing into the countryside or huddling in cellars, waiting it out. The Loyalists of New Haven, meanwhile, welcomed the soldiers—although they discovered the invaders, particularly the Hessians, did not always discriminate, robbing and abusing rebel and Loyalist alike. But the next day, when witnesses saw "in the dim morning light, the British officers driving their intoxicated soldiers across the green on the way to the Wharf," Loyalists faced the prospect of remaining to face the wrath of their neighbors. The British invited the city Tories to sail with them, an offer four families accepted. The men reembarked on their ships, fired a few cannonballs at the town and sailed back toward New York. They left behind them twenty-seven dead citizens, seventeen wounded and more than £24,893 in damages.[152]

It had been a hit-and-run strike. Both Brigadier General Garth and Major General William Tryon, the former governor of New York, feared being surrounded by militia from nearby towns, which had begun to collect and organize a counteroffensive. Any attack on them in the outskirts opened the risk of the British being cut off from their ships in the harbor. Having succeeded in their mission, they retreated back into the Sound, burning a few homes but leaving the town's architecture relatively unscathed. The stores at the wharf and the barracks of a fort were also burned.[153]

"About four o'clock the next morning," wrote the Reverend Andrew Eliot of Christ's Church, Fairfield's Congregational church, "the approach of the fleet was announced by the firing of a gun from a small fort we have on Grover's Hill." This was a twenty-five-man battery on the southernmost point of land between Black Rock Harbor and Ash Creek, established by order of Trumbull and the council in February 1776 to defend the harbor. The fleet didn't stop, however, but kept going. The townspeople on the beach anxiously watched them pass to the west. A fog rolled in, and the ships were lost to sight.[154]

Then, between nine and ten o'clock, the fog withdrew like a magician's cape to reveal the entire fleet anchored south of the Mill River—right where the town had beaten back the Long Island Loyalists.

They sat there until four in the afternoon. Then "they began to land their troops a little to the east of Kensie's Point, at a place called the Pines. From thence the troops marched along the beach until they came to a lane opposite the centre of town, through which they proceeded."[155]

The town militia gathered near Kensie's Point, thinking the British would attempt, as the Loyalists had, to land on the shore east of Mill River's mouth. Realizing they were disembarking closer to town instead,

In July 1989, Fairfield hosted a reenactment of the 1779 attack on the town. Here British redcoats march up Beach Road toward the green, just as they did 210 years before. *Fairfield Museum and History Center.*

the militia retreated to the center green. By this time, the British came to modern-day Beach Road, which runs perpendicular to the beach, and began marching up the road toward the center of town. Cannon fire from the fort at Black Rock prevented them from going any farther east along the shore. As the British column marched, the militia, stationed at the top of Beach Road, "gave them such a warm reception with a field-piece, which threw both round and grape-shot, and with their musketry, as quite disconcerted them for some time." There is no mention of who manned the cannon, but it may be guessed that its crew was the same as before: Smedley, Sturges and Mr. Hazzard.[156]

British discipline held firm, and the column forced the militiamen to retreat into the hills north of town, leaving downtown nearly deserted as the British reached the green between the courthouse and the meeting house.

A few women, some of whom were of the most respectable families and characters, tarried with a view of saving their property. They imagined their sex and character would avail to such a purpose. They put some confidence in the generosity of an enemy who were once famed for generosity and politeness; and thought that kind treatment and submissive behavior would secure them against harsh treatment and rough usage. Alas! they were miserably mistaken.[157]

The three British divisions paraded on the green, led by General Tryon. Only after the first house was torched did Tryon read a prepared statement, similar to the one given at New Haven:

That owing to their delusion in hoping for independence they were deceiving themselves; that the existence of a single habitation on your defenceless coast ought to be a constant proof of your ingratitude. Therefore we offer you a refuge against the distress which you universally acknowledge broods with increasing & intolerable weight over all your country; & that whosoever shall be found, & remain in peace at his usual place of residence, shall be shielded from any insult either to his property, excepting such as bear offices, either civil or military, under your present usurped government, of whom it will be further required that they shall give proof of their penitence & voluntary submission, when they shall partake of the like community. But those whose folly & obstinacy may slight this favorable warning must take notice that they are not to expect a continuance of that lenity which their inveteracy would not now render blameless.[158]

A copy reached its way to Colonel Whiting, rallying the militia and troops north of town. His reply to Tryon was more laconic: "Connecticut has nobly dared to take up arms against the cruel despotism of Britain, and as the flames have now preceded your flag, they will persist to oppose to the utmost that power exerted against injured innocence."[159]

As night fell over Fairfield, the women who stayed behind to protect their homes learned the value of Tryon's promises.

The testimony of Jane Bulkley:

A number of officers & men came to my house, & received such refreshment as they required, & said that persons who staid in their houses, should be safe in person & property, & at their request I went & milked my cow & gave them the milk, whereupon the cow was led away by them & killed; my house was fir'd five times & I extinguished it.[160]

The testimony of Mary Beers:

*A picket of Hessians in General Garth's division broke into our house
& thereupon I came out of the cellar with two small children & a negro
child, & on opening the cellar door, they cried out, Kill her, kill her, &
came at me with a number of fixed bayonets: I begged & intreated,
implored & prayed, to spare my life & run back down the cellar &
opened the out cellar door & went into door yard, with the afores'd three
children.*[161]

The testimony of Eunice, wife of Thaddeus Burr:

*By the time that the main body of the enemy had got up to the court
house, instead of the once humane & polite Britons, a pack of the most
barbarous ruffians came rushing into the house, & repeatedly accosted
me with you Dam Rebel where is your husband, he is a selectman—at
the same time striping me of my buckles, taring down the curtains of my
bed, breaking the frame of my dressing glass, pulling out the draws of
my table & desk; & after taking what they could find, they then went
up stairs & proceeded much in the same manner.*

An officer arrived and ordered the men out of the house, but "no sooner
were one set out, but another came in, calling for syder, breaking down
the china, stone & glass ware in the closets & where ever they found it."
General Tryon appeared, demanding paperwork, which Eunice delivered,
but once he left, she was chased into the yard "& there committed myself
to that God, whose protection & mercy is beyond the reach of such cruel
monsters. They however were permitted to pursue me, throw me upon
the ground, & search me, pulling & taring at my cloths from me in a most
barbarious manner, no intreaties or persuasions prevailing upon them to
desist." She was again saved by the fortuitous approach of the officer.[162]

The testimony of Lucretia Readfield:

*Thro' the whole night the soldiers went where they pleased and did as
they pleased, without any restraint from their officers so far as I could
observe, & they came to my house & abused me with abusive & insulting*

language, carriage & behaviour: They destroyed the furniture in the house, & attempted, with threats & promises, to prevail upon me to yield to their unchaste & unlawful desires. I obstinately denied them my body: three men then & there appeared intent to compass their wicked design, seized me & dragged me to the bed & attempted violence, but thanks to God there appeared that instant to come two persons who rescued me from their violence, one of whom told me he had been a prisoner in this town, & that he had received great civility from the inhabitants, & that he had an opinion of their being a worthy kind people, & those two persons protected me thro' the remainder of the night.

The former prisoner was likely a Loyalist, jailed in Fairfield as a person dangerous and inimical to the Revolution.[163]

Not every man fled, and a few fought back:

A Mr. Tucker fired from his shop on the parade at the whole army only a few rods distant, & was wounded by them in the shoulder & taken prisoner. Mr. Parsons fired from a chamber into the road & killed a British officer; then running out the back door made his escape. The enemy coming into the house found an old negro bedridden; they said it was him, he declared it was not; they put the bayonet into him & burnt the house.

On the outskirts of town, farther from the green, the British and their mercenaries were less secure. "Our people on the heights back of the town were joined by numbers, but not equal to the numbers of the enemy," wrote the Reverend Eliot. "They were skirmishing all the evening, part of the night, and the next morning. The enemy were several times disconcerted and driven from their outposts."[164]

The conflagration lit up the night's sky, as the drunken soldiers and mercenaries ran through the streets, grabbing anything of value, consuming every kind of liquor. "The town burnt all night—a cloud seemed to remain fixed in the west, from which issued frequent flashes of lightning." Nearly every house and barn was put to the flame. Tryon issued exemptions for certain buildings—Burr's home, the house of the Reverend Eliot, the Anglican and Congregational churches—and ordered sentries to protect them. But with sunrise, what order the British maintained evaporated completely. "No sooner had the horn blew," testified Eunice Burr, "I suppose for the whole to retreat, my centrys went off & a band of those savage creatures were left as a rear guard to compleat the destruction." These were jagers, Hessian light infantry. "The rear-guard, which behaved in so scandalous a manner," wrote the Reverend Eliot, "were chiefly German troops, called Yaugers. They carry a small rifle-gun and fight in a skulking manner, like our Indians." Some rushed into Burr's house and attacked the women who had sought shelter there. "Seeing a number more of them come into the gate. I once more took courage, went out & intreated them to spare the house; told them that I had General Tryon's protection in writing; upon which they damned the general & protection too & tore it from me." Burr fled. Her whole house was devoured by the flames, as were the Reverend Eliot's and the two churches.[165]

At eight o'clock in the morning, the British began their retreat to the ships. What they had feared in New Haven came to pass in Fairfield: a running fight to the beach as the regrouped militia poured out of the hills. "The militia followed these bloody incendiaries to the place of embarkation, and galled them considerably," wrote the Reverend Eliot. "About noon the enemy returned on board at Kenzy's Point, & were pursued through the burning houses by enraged inhabitants," wrote William Wheeler in his journal. "The roar of the small arms was continued like the roll of a drum."[166]

The militia cornered them on the beach, but the British had knocked down all the stone walls nearby, giving the Fairfielders little protection. The British kept a covering fire to protect the soldiers loading into the boats.

Meanwhile, the British sent a row galley mounting an eighteen-pound cannon toward Black Rock Harbor but were repulsed by the battery on the point. The two forces blasted away at each other without damage, but the curtain of cannonballs was enough to stop the galley. Prevented from proceeding farther, the British turned back. This saved the wharves, storehouses and captain's houses of Black Rock, including Ebenezer Bartram's.[167]

The enemy fleet escaped to Huntington, on Long Island's north shore, where it then recrossed the Sound and burned Norwalk on July 11. The British lost more men than the Fairfielders—"About 40 of the enemy were found dead & 8 or 10 of ours"—but the town suffered the graver loss. Only eleven houses remained in the whole village, their fires "extinguished by our people who followed close at the heels of the English." More than two hundred buildings lay in ash.[168]

Samuel Smedley and his wife, Esther, lost everything except their lives and the clothes they wore. Two houses, a barn, a workshop, clothing, provisions, furniture—valued at £795, more than the entire captors' share of *John*—were now rubble and smoking ruin. Worse was the loss to history. During his time on *Defence*, Smedley surely wrote letters to his wife, relating the small moments between battles, the anecdotes, the privations. Not just the business details of paying wages and stocking bread onboard but also the experiences and observations that paint a portrait of a life. Lost.

It would be a hard winter for Fairfield, "the most terrible but one (1740) ever seen since the settlement of New England." Esther Smedley probably went next door to live with her uncle, Andrew Rowland, whose wife endured the fury and drunkenness of the enemy to preserve it. "A British officer with his men went to fire it, when she told them of a favor she had done years before to a British officer, and in consequence her house was spared." The house stands there still. With no children of her own, Esther would have been a great asset in helping the Rowlands and fellow refugees prepare for the coming winter.[169]

Samuel Smedley didn't plan on passing the winter in Fairfield. Before, the war had been something apart, something separate for Smedley, an event that happened in New York or Boston or on the water, something to be fought for idealism, for virtue. Now it had come to his home. War had entered Fairfield, marched down its streets, burned his and his neighbors' houses, killed men he knew by name and assaulted their wives. Losing the war meant he, Fairfield, Connecticut, America could expect more of the same. But what could they to do? *Defence* was wrecked, the state navy obliterated, the Continental Navy just a handful of ships.

There was another option.

Chapter 8

"TO KEEP BODY & SOUL TOGETHER"

S everal Merchants and others have petitioned the Congress for leave to fit out privateers to Cruize against British Vessels," wrote Joseph Hewes, secretary of the navy, to a friend on March 20, 1776. "It was granted yesterday."[170]

There were no more Connecticut state ships for Smedley to sail on. *Defence* had wrecked in March 1779. The state's galleys—*Whiting*, *Shark* and *Crane*—had all been captured or burned by spring 1777. The sloop *Schuyler* was also captured later that year. The old *Defence*, the original *Lily Ann*, was captured in 1778, the same year the schooner *Spy* was taken returning from Brest, where it delivered the ratified alliance treaty between the United States and France. *Oliver Cromwell*, captained by his friend, Timothy Parker, had been seized in June 1779 off Sandy Hook, New Jersey. Even the new sloop *Guilford*—the one Smedley had turned down—was gone; it had been caught in New Haven Harbor when the British invaded.

But there were privateers. After resolving to issue letters of marque and reprisal in March 1776, the Continental Congress on April 3 established the terms of the commissions. Privateers, upon posting a bond ($5,000 if the vessel's tonnage was one hundred tons or less, $10,000 if it was bigger), had permission to "attack, subdue, and take all ships and other vessels belonging to the inhabitants of Great Britain on the high seas" but had to follow strict rules of conduct to distinguish them from pirates and thieves. Ships had to be brought in and libeled in the admiralty court with their paperwork and cargo intact; prisoners could not be abused, tortured, ransomed or their clothing or personal belongings stripped; and friendly vessels could not be attacked. Failure to follow the terms meant forfeiture of the bond and revocation of the government's legal protection— meaning the malefactors could be sued for damages by the victims.[171]

Unlike with the Continental or state navies, the government didn't take any cut of the prizes. The privateers posted the bonds and fitted themselves at their own expense, and all the profits were theirs to keep. The division of prizes was individual to each venture, but the general rule was half for the owners and investors and half for the crew. It is doubtful any seaman would sail for less. Crewmembers usually were not paid wages as they were on the state ships, instead working solely for the prize money—if any—received after the voyage had ended; but again, the specific terms were delineated in the ship's articles each sailor signed before joining an expedition.

Some colonies issued their own letters of marque and reprisal; Massachusetts began doing so in November 1775, before the Continental Congress. Connecticut did not issue any privateering commissions under its own authority. All its privateers sailed with congressional letters. Congress would issue blank commissions—printed at a press and then signed in bulk by committee members, with spaces for the ship's details to be filled in later—and then disperse them to "the general assemblies, conventions, and councils or committees of safety of the United Colonies, to be by them filled up and delivered to the persons intending to fit out such private ships of war." (Privateering would later be relegated from a military responsibility to a pecuniary one. In October 1777, the Congress issued a fresh batch of one hundred blank commissions to be distributed by the Committee of Commerce.) The first Connecticut privateer of the Revolution was rigged and readied out of Black Rock Harbor in April 1776. Thaddeus Burr was among its backers.[172]

On February 18, 1780, the privateer *Recovery* received its letter of marque in New London. Samuel Smedley, John Grinnell and Joseph Williams posted the $20,000 bond. Williams also owned the ship. *Recovery* mounted sixteen six-pounders, just like *Defence*, built in Rhode Island. After making sure his town and wife were secure, Smedley probably spent the following fall and winter working to assemble the venture and hire crew. He had inherited several parcels of undeveloped land from his father, and with his house and outbuildings destroyed—presumably along with any assets within that weren't stolen by the invaders—he may have used the deeds as collateral for his part of the bond.

Five days after the commission, the local newspaper advertised that "the Privateer Ship RECOVERY, commanded by Samuel Smedley is now completely ready for sea" and informed those who had previously engaged to grab their bags and go aboard. With Smedley's reputation and a privateer's prize division, signing men was not the problem it had been on the state ship. James Angel, who had served as Smedley's first lieutenant on *Defence*, repeated his role onboard *Recovery*. The names of several other former *Defence* sailors turned up on the crew list as well.[173]

By March, *Recovery* was underway. This time, Smedley initiated a new strategy, one that combined targeting West Indian traders but without sailing so far from home. With the seizure of New York City by the British in August 1776, significant traffic developed between the port and the British colonies in the West Indies. The rest of America may have been in rebellion, but the British in New York still drank rum. So instead of dipping down to the teen latitudes and grabbing merchant marines coming from England, now Smedley simply had to hover off the eastern shore of New Jersey and net them as they came north, aiming for the Lower Bay. Such was the case with the sloop *Hope*, en route to New York from St. Kitts with a cargo of eighty-four puncheons of rum. *Recovery* captured and sent her into New London on March 14.

But the year was 1780, not 1776. The British had become firmly established in New York and ruled its waters. Nine days later, on March 23, Smedley sighted HMS *Galatea* bearing down on them. At twenty guns, *Galatea* was relatively matched with *Recovery*'s sixteen. The problem was that *Galatea* was accompanied by a cutter, the vessel "formerly Cuningham." Smedley could handle one warship; two was dicier.[174]

Smedley gave the orders to turn south and run. They had been lingering off Sandy Hook, the same area where Parker and *Oliver Cromwell* were taken. Now the three ships raced down the New Jersey coast for a hundred miles, the two Britishers inching closer. Finally, about eighty-five miles due east of Cape May, Smedley struck *Recovery*'s colors.

There is no record of the battle—or even if there was one, although it's difficult to imagine there wasn't some kind of engagement—nor of damages, injuries or deaths. Ship and crew were dragged into New York, the *Recovery* libeled four days later.

As the commander of the vessel, Smedley was deposed in the New York Court of Vice Admiralty. He kept his responses to just the facts. He identified himself as being born in Connecticut, "a subject of the United States of America." Other questions about simple, noncontroversial points—yes, he was the commander; the ship was owned by Joseph Williams and Company, as stated on the letter of marque; et cetera—he answered succinctly. The majority of questions he refused to answer: "this Deponent saith that he cannot materially depose."[175]

And then, afterward, Smedley and his ninety-four officers and crewmen were "all delivered to Prison Ship at New York."[176]

Opposite Manhattan's Lower East Side, sandwiched between the Brooklyn and Williamsburg Bridges, lies the Brooklyn Navy Yard. But earlier it was known as Wallabout Bay, a marshy inlet of mud flats at low tide. In a channel there rested the British prison ships. The largest and most infamous was *Jersey*, a former sixty-four-gun ship of the line that had been stripped down to a massive coffin. Masts, spars and rigging had been removed, leaving only a flagstaff and the bowsprit. The ports were nailed shut. Thousands of prisoners, sailors all, were crammed within, freezing in the winter and so hot in the summer that the inmates stripped naked and panted for breath. Smedley and his men, like most prisoners, were "Victual'd at 2/3d Allowance," meaning they were granted two-thirds of the ration given to Royal Navy seamen. The food was rotten, full of vermin; the water had to be strained before being drunk. In addition to *Jersey*, there were eight other ships in the bay used for the same purpose.[177]

Before he was captain of *Oliver Cromwell*, Timothy Parker had served as first lieutenant aboard the Connecticut state schooner *Spy*. He was the prize master of *Hope*, taken by *Spy*, when the *Hope* was retaken by the British and brought into New York. Parker and five members of his prize crew were thrown into Wallabout Bay's first prison ship, *Whitby*, in late 1776. "There are more than two Hundred and fifty prisoners of us on board this ship (some of which are Sick and without the least assistance from Physician, Drugg, or Medicine)," wrote Parker to Trumbull, asking for an exchange. Parker and the rest were "allowed only to walk the main deck from about Sun Rising till Sun Sett, at which time we are ordered below deck and suffered only one at once to come on deck to do what nature requires, and sometimes we have been even Denied that, and been obliged to make use of tubbs & bucketts below deck… to great prejudice of all our healths." Ebenezer Bartram Jr., Smedley's cousin and sailing mate, did time in the prison ships, returning home via a flag in March 1781. Bartram's sons, Joseph and Ebenezer, were also imprisoned in *Jersey*. "While in Prison, their allowance was scarce enough to keep body & soul together—their bedclothing was so scant that one half had to walk in their shirts while the rest slept, & those that were delicate perished. In those long & dismal nights they were enveloped in total darkness, being allowed no candles." The Bartram boys managed to escape during the bitter winter of 1780. They and five others fled the ship and "waited on the ice for about 40 more. They not coming, they took to their heels, amidst a shower of bullets which were fir'd from the surrounding guardships, & made for the land." After further trials, the men found their way home to Fairfield.[178]

"I beg you wold send Stanton Hazard down as soon as possible as I shall remain hear till he comes," wrote one prisoner, a privateer captain named Dan Scovell. "I have been striped of all my clothes my Officers and Men am all well but on board the Prisin ship very much crowded." Scovell had also been captured by *Galatea* and its cutter after a tight chase lasting seven hours. Scovell threw ten of his guns overboard and started tossing the hogsheads full of water when the cutter cut across his bow, pinning him between her and *Galatea*. The same tactic may have trapped *Recovery*. Now Scovell wrote to a friend in New London, pleading to be exchanged for Captain Stanton Hazard, a Rhode Island officer in the Royal Navy. Hazard's vessel had been captured by a privateer, and he was currently paroled to the house of his sister in Narragansett. "Send down hazard I beg let the cost of a flag com on me the small pox is on board the Prisin Ship."[179]

In his letter, Scovell mentioned that Smedley had also been taken by *Galatea*. Trumbull arranged with Rhode Island governor William Greene to exchange Hazard for Scovell, as well as another prisoner they had, Lieutenant Lock, for Smedley. Greene agreed to the bargain, "upon conditions that your Excellency will give this State your Assurances to do them the like favour when ever there may be a necessity for it."[180]

A flag was set—the flag of truce where prisoners were exchanged—and Hazard and Lock sailed to New York. But by the time they arrived, the two Americans were gone. "Smedley & Scovel were sent out before we knew of this flag," reads a cryptic line written by the commissary-general of prisoners on May 11. They may have been paroled (Scovell mentioned possibly being paroled to Long Island). To go on parole, a person had to swear to quit hostilities in the war, whereupon he was ordered to stay somewhere under the observation of local authorities, as in the cases of Ebenezer Hall and Isaac Tomlinson, the two Connecticut Tories whom Trumbull and the council paroled in January 1777. How close the scrutiny was depended on the perceived trustworthiness of the parolee. If paroled to Long Island, there was nothing keeping Smedley there except a coerced promise and his Loyalist hosts, who had to sleep sometime.[181]

On October 10, 1780, the sloop *Hibernia* was commissioned as privateer in New London with Samuel Smedley as her commander. Smedley, along with Joseph Howland and Thomas Coit, posted the $20,000 bond; Howland and Coit were also the sloop's owners. Smedley likely had been able to retrieve the bond money for *Recovery*—privateer bonds were simply leashes to keep them from tilting into full-scale piracy, so loss of *Recovery* didn't mean loss of the bond—and used it toward *Hibernia*. But *Hibernia* was far more modest than either *Defence* or *Recovery*: ten guns and a full complement of forty-seven men. Some of the money spent on outfitting *Recovery* had been Smedley's own, and with that investment gone, both his ambitions and wallet were diminished.

With James Angel and the rest of *Recovery*'s crew still cooling in the prison ships, Smedley needed a new crew. Robert McKown was master. Other familiar "gentlemen volunteers" appear on the articles as well, including *Defence* sailor John Wasson (by now married to the niece of Ebenezer Bartram Jr.) and Bartram's eighteen-year-old son, Ebenezer III. Unlike with *Recovery*, a copy exists of *Hibernia*'s articles of agreement. It is remarkable what little difference stands between Smedley's covenant with his sailors and those from the age of the buccaneers. Loss of an arm or leg, "or be otherwise so disabled as not to earn his Bread," was compensated with £1,000 onboard *Hibernia*. Under his English letter of marque, Henry Morgan granted "six hundred pieces of eight or six slaves" for a lost leg or hand. With Smedley, "whoever shall first enter an Enemy's Ship, after orders for boarding is issued, he shall receive three hundred pounds as a Recompense for his Valour." Morgan rewarded the same with fifty pieces of eight. And, as captain, Smedley was entitled to eight shares of the half prize awarded to officers and crew—the exact same portion given to captains sailing under Morgan's flag a century prior.[182]

Yet the sailors of *Hibernia* would never have a chance to divide any spoils. Just two weeks after its commissioning, on October 25, *Hibernia* was chased and captured by HMS *Hussar* at thirty-three degrees north latitude, off the Carolinas. Smedley may have been resuming his old tactics by returning to the West Indies, or he may have decided to travel closer to the source of the produce flowing into New York but beyond the city's halo of British warships. Either way, crew and sloop were packed to New York for prosecution and libel.

There, the absurd provenience of *Hibernia*'s ownership was unraveled. Three local merchants came forward claiming that *Hibernia* was theirs and filed to repossess it. Smedley testified that he had first become acquainted with the sloop at Norwich, but he understood it had been built in Virginia. While sailing out of New York, *Hibernia* had been taken by an American privateer and brought into New London. From there it was moved to Norwich and outfitted as a privateer. Now the New York merchants had it back, at least temporarily. Some ten months later, in August 1781, *Hibernia* would again be sent into New London, having since been outfitted as a privateer under a British commission but taken yet again by Americans.[183]

Smedley and his crew were consigned on October 29 to "Charon prison," perhaps the HMS *Charon*. The British bureaucrats must have realized this was the second time they had snared the recalcitrant Smedley in a single year. There would be no parole this time. In December, a British ship arrived in New London from New York with an exchange of one hundred prisoners. "By this Flag we are informed," reads a newspaper write-up of the event, "that all Officers of Privateers should be sent to England; and that in Consequence of this Order, not long since, a Number of Officers were sent to England, among whom was Capt. Smedley, from this Port."[184]

Prizes Captured by Samuel Smedley

Date of Capture	Name
Sunday, May 12, 1776	*Life Guard* (?)
Sunday, June 16, 1776	*George*
Sunday, June 16, 1776	*Annabella*
Tuesday, June 18, 1776	*Lord Howe*
August-September 1776	*John*
before Tuesday, October 22, 1776	*Guinea Man*
August-October 1776	*Sally*
Wednesday, March 12, 1777	*Lydia* (?)
Sunday, March 16, 1777	*Anna*
before Saturday, March 22, 1777	*Grog*
before Saturday, April 19, 1777	*Swift*
Wednesday, April 15, 1778	*Cyrus*
Friday, June 19, 1778	*Governor Tonyn's Revenge*
Friday, June 19, 1778	*Ranger*
before Sunday, March 14, 1780	*Hope*

Smedley's privateering career was over before it even began, with just one prize to his credit. He had been aboard the state ship *Defence* for all fourteen of her captures, half of which occurred while he was captain. And only three of those fourteen were Royal Navy. If only he had been able to bring that same fortune to *Recovery* and *Hibernia*; if only he had been as good at taking merchantmen as a privateer as he had been commanding a state ship. Or had *Defence* been a privateer venture all along—and this was just the end of Smedley's run?

Chapter 9

"Samuel Smedley of Connecticut Ran Away"

M ill Prison lay on a headland outside of the town of Plymouth, England. The oldest of the prison buildings was built in the early years of the eighteenth century; before its construction, there had been a cluster of windmills on the site. The prison was a two-story stone building. There was an office, a kitchen and a hospital with a yard. The whole was surrounded by a double set of walls, with broken glass set in the mortar on top of the east and south lengths. Two guards stood watch in the yard by day and four at night, while another four marched watches beyond the walls. Two sentries were posted on each floor of the prison house.[185]

In December 1780, the sixty-four-gun *Yarmouth* was ordered to transport a number of naval and privateer officers from New York across the Atlantic to Mill Prison. The dates suggest Smedley and *Hibernia*'s master, Robert McKown, may have been among the seventy-one Americans aboard. It was a brutal event. Told by the sailors they were being taken to England to be hanged—because the American government was not recognized by Britain, the American seamen were considered pirates—the men were packed into the lower hold, below the water line, in a chamber twelve by twenty feet by three feet high. For fifty-three days, they were kept in the darkness without ventilation or exercise or sanitation, given bad food and rotten water. Eleven died during the passage.[186]

Having survived the crossing, Smedley and McKown were committed to the Mill Prison in March 1781. Conditions there were better than onboard the prison ships—prisoners were issued a hammock, straw mattress, blanket and pillow and also had an annual clothing ration—but food distribution was so uneven that inmates could count on just enough food for one meal a day. American prisoners were issued seven pounds of bread a week while French and Spanish prisoners, housed separately, were granted ten and a half pounds. The reason for this, the Americans were told, was because the latter two groups were considered lawful prisoners of war, while the Americans were classified as rebels, which, according to a 1745 law, meant they were only entitled to the lesser amount.[187]

"Captain Smedley's lady received a letter from Him dated at Mill Prison, in Plymouth, England, May 25, 1781," wrote Connecticut militia colonel Christopher Leffingwell to Governor Trumbull in September 1781. "He represents his condition very disagreeable, cruelly treated, half starved & half naked. She begs of me and her friends this way, to devise some means to procure his release, which I most heartily wish might be effected."[188]

Fresh air and movement in the yard allowed Smedley to rebuild his body. Prisoners were allowed to receive funds from home or from English charitable societies. Some prisoners would fashion scraps of wood into ladles, spoons and boxes for barter or sale with locals through the bars of the front gate. Another source of income was the tireless effort of Benjamin Franklin, who worked nonstop not only in forging peace treaties with France and other foreign powers but also to secure the release of his fellow Americans. "The late practice of sending to England prisoners taken in America has greatly augmented the number of those unfortunate men and proportionally increased the expense of relieving them," Franklin wrote from Passy to Thomas McKean, the president of Congress. "The allowance I have made to them of sixpence each per week during the summer though small amounts to a considerable sum and during the winter I shall be obliged to double if not treble it." It wasn't just the inmates that absorbed his time and finances—escapees cost money, too. In Amsterdam, John Adams's funds dwindled. "My loan rests as it was, at a few thousand guilders, which, by the advice of Dr. Franklin, I reserve for the relief of our countrymen who escape from prison in England in distress."[189]

Prisoners could use money to buy food, clothes and toiletries. Or the money could be used toward the dominant pastime: escape. An attempt was made by one group to go through the prison sewer to the river, but the plan was thwarted by a double grate of bars. Tunneling was also popular. Most tries involved bribing guards and going over the wall. Joshua Barney, a lieutenant in the American navy, developed a friendship with one of the guards. By accumulating small sums, he was able to purchase a British officer's uniform from the guard, which, on the appointed day, Barney wore under his great coat. When most of the sentries were at lunch, Barney clambered over the first wall with the help of an accomplice, and landing between the two walls, threw away his coat, paid the colluding guard four guineas and walked out the front gate in disguise.[190]

Which of these methods Smedley used is unknown. His record from Mill Prison simply says, "Samuel Smedley of Connecticut ran away."[191]

The last months of 1781 were a migraine for Benjamin Franklin in Paris. Having spent a large sum on purchasing various goods and wares—"all articles exceedingly wanted in America"—Franklin had entrusted their portage to Alexander Gillon, the commodore of the South Carolina navy, with whom Smedley had captured the two St. Augustine privateers in 1778. Gillon, in Europe in command of the state frigate *South Carolina*, had conceived a plan to bring a fat load of needed commodities home to America. Franklin, though "having little confidence in Captain Gillon's management," feared that Gillon acting on his own would embarrass the United States and fray its tenuous alliances, so he extended £10,000 toward the enterprise, thereby hoping to maintain some control over it. Because there was still room in *South Carolina*'s hold, Franklin authorized further purchases to fill the space. He was then shocked to receive bills tallying not £5,000, as he expected, but rather £50,000. He first refused to pay them, but when he was told the goods were already onboard the ships and that unloading and selling them would incur further expense and humiliation, Franklin went fur hat in hand to the French ministers and begged for more money to pay for it all.[192]

It got worse. The officers of *South Carolina* complained the ship was overburdened, too clumsy to fight with no room for provisions or sailors. So two other ships were hired to divide the cargo among them—which

Gillon promptly deserted to go take prizes in the Caribbean. Because the two ships had contracted to sail in convoy with *South Carolina* and because the Atlantic churned with English warships and privateers, the shipowners demanded Franklin either pay for additional gunners and marines to defend the ships or buy the ships outright. Franklin had no money to do either and refused to lose face again in front of the French. On top of everything else, Gillon had run up personal debts with the shipowners, and they held the cargo as collateral until these were repaid, notwithstanding the fact that the goods were owned by the States. "This piece of business has been managed as ill as any that has ever been done for Congress in Europe," wrote Adams. Franklin was more blunt: "It has been, and will be a villainous affair from beginning to end."[193]

Even if Franklin could disentangle the goods from their detention, he still faced another problem: how to ship them safely to America. What they needed was a responsible American sea captain, a merchant marine with battle experience who wouldn't flake on them like Gillon.

"I wrote to Nantes to Engage Captain Smedley, who is every way qualified for the business," wrote Thomas Barclay in Amsterdam, "and who I am inform'd is on his way hither."[194]

After wandering away from Mill Prison, Smedley reappeared in December 1781 in Brest, France, where he became acquainted with David Salisbury Franks, a government officer who had couriered letters from America to John Jay and Franklin. Franks and Smedley shared something in common: both were having trouble finding passage back to the States. "With much difficulty I got a promise of a Pass for Capt. Smedley to go to L'orient, he has been waiting here a long time by the ministers desire," wrote Franks to William Temple Franklin, Benjamin's grandson and personal secretary. Both Franks and Smedley intended to hitch a ride home on the *St. James* sailing out of L'Orient.[195]

This mention of Smedley to his grandson might have been the aspirin to Benjamin Franklin's pains over the Gillon affair. Both Franks and Smedley went from L'Orient to Nantes, by the *St. James* or otherwise, where their paths diverged: Franks on a mission for Jay to Spain, Smedley to Passy. There Smedley met with the elder Franklin. The captain clearly passed the job interview because Franklin entrusted him with a packet of letters to Adams in Amsterdam—though Franklin complained in another letter, "Smedley did not leave Paris so soon as I expected." Smedley would hardly be the last American to linger in the City of Lights.[196]

In Amsterdam, Thomas Barclay, the American consul to France, engaged a ship from Ostend called *Heer Adams*, sixteen guns, which Smedley inspected in late April and found suitable. With the financial impediments resolved (Gillon's shenanigans would eventually be sorted out by a congressional committee), the cargo was transferred from the two Dutch ships to *Heer Adams* and a ten-gun brigantine, *General Green*, which would sail in convoy to the United States. To man them, Barclay sent out a call to any escaped or exchanged American prisoners. And so that Smedley might "make prize of any of the Enemys vessells that possibly may fall in his way," Barclay and Franklin commissioned him with a third letter of marque.[197]

Smedley and *Heer Adams* would loiter in Amsterdam until late June, the cargo aboard but "the Captains sickness and want of hands made all kind of hurry useless." He was still recovering from his imprisonment. On the twenty-seventh, Barclay informed Franklin that *Heer Adams* was over the sand banks at the river's mouth "and will in a few days be able to put to Sea" after collecting a few more sailors.[198]

It was an uneventful crossing, no prizes taken. Smedley was probably grateful for it. He had had enough adventure to last a lifetime but at the cost of his health and his home and without laying eyes on his wife for almost a year. The sight of the American coastline must have been welcome not just to him but to all the former prisoners onboard, the goal for which they had all worked and suffered. The United States Smedley returned to was subtly different than those he had left. Before, it had been a country where the war was going badly. Now it was a place where, on October 19, 1781, General Charles Cornwallis had surrendered at Yorktown, Virginia.

"Dear Sir," wrote Robert Livingston to John Jay from Philadelphia on September 12, 1782,

> *We yesterday received letters from Mr. Adams by Captain Smedley, who brought out the goods left by Commodore Gillon. These were the first advices that had reached us from Europe since your short note of the 14th of May. You will easily believe that this neglect is borne here with some degree of impatience, particularly at this interesting period, when we learn that a negociation for a peace has commenced...[199]*

Chapter 10
"AMIDST THE GREATEST OF TROUBLES"

On a Friday afternoon in October 1789, a carriage drawn by four horses bumped down the King's Highway through Fairfield. Crowds thronged the road, waving and cheering; red, white and blue flags and bunting draped from the rails and windows of the houses—well, from those homes that had been rebuilt over the previous decade. "The Destructive evidences of British cruelty are yet visible both in Norwalk and Fairfield," wrote the carriage's occupant in his diary, "as there are the chimneys of many burnt houses standing in them yet."[200]

The carriage rolled to a stop outside of a town tavern. Immediately the crowd closed around it. Six servants piled off, lowered the step, and held open the carriage door. Out came Tobias Lear and Major William Jackson, aides to the final figure inside. He exited last: His Excellency George Washington, president of the United States of America.

Washington had left his wife in New York to travel to Boston, a tour made ostensibly to measure the mood of the populace toward its new Constitution and president but also for Washington's relief of mind and health—a vacation. In Fairfield, where Washington and his party "dined and lodged," he was entertained by the town patriarchs, people like Thaddeus Burr, Andrew Rowland and, of course, Samuel Smedley. It may have been from Smedley that Washington learned, "The principal export from Norwalk and Fairfield is Horses and Cattle—salted Beef

The reconstructed home of Samuel Smedley, built after the burning of 1779 and believed to have been based on the original. From a drawing courtesy of Thomas B. Osborne. *Fairfield Museum and History Center.*

and Pork—Lumber and Indian Corn, to the West Indies, and in a small degree Wheat and Flour."[201]

Since the end of the war, Smedley had returned to running the West Indies trade between Connecticut and the Caribbean, only this time as a merchant marine. He commanded the brigantine *Greenfield* out of Black Rock Harbor, bankrolled by members of the Bradley family and, later, his half brother, John Smedley. With cargoes of mainly horses, barrels of onions and potatoes and wood planks, boards and staves, he returned with rum, molasses and sugar, along with small amounts of coffee and indigo. Patterns of commerce had returned to what they had been before the war, only this time it was legal, done without having to post bonds in New London, and the sea captains were allowed to trade wherever they wanted with whomever they wanted—or, at least, in those foreign ports open to Americans.

In 1789, perhaps as a result of meeting him in Fairfield, Washington appointed Smedley as the first customs house collector for the Federal District Port of Fairfield. This included a broad swath of coastline, from

Today the chandlery founded in 1772 by Samuel Smedley and Samuel Sturges is the Fayerweather Yacht Club. The original posts and beams are still present. *Jackson Kuhl.*

A sign outside the Fayerweather Yacht Club. *Jackson Kuhl.*

Stratford down to the New York border, making him responsible for collecting duties from every ship that docked in Stamford, Norwalk, Fairfield and so on. Smedley surrendered seafaring and held the job until his death.

James Angel must have escaped the prison ships or been exchanged after being captured alongside Smedley in *Recovery*. By July 1781, he was in command of a sixteen-gun privateer brig, *Minerva* (not the same *Minerva* that briefly had been a state ship in 1775). She took at least one prize, a brig named *Rose*.[202]

The prison ships seem to have permanently scarred Ebenezer Bartram Jr. He died in January 1783, less than two years after being exchanged, at the age of fifty-two. But he left behind a host of sons and nephews who followed him into the maritime trade, including his son, Joseph, who died at sea while returning from the West Indies onboard *Greenfield* with Smedley. The Bartrams stamped their name on Black Rock—today there is a Bartram Avenue—and some of their houses still stand in the neighborhood.

After a two-hour engagement with four Britishers off New Jersey in June 1779, Timothy Parker struck *Oliver Cromwell*'s colors and was cast for the second time into a New York prison ship. He was exchanged in August 1779. He went on to command two privateers: *Scourge*, twenty guns, in May 1781, and *Prudence*, ten guns, in September 1782. He returned to the merchant-marine trade at the war's end and died in May 1797.[203]

Overwhelmed by superior guns, Seth Harding surrendered *Confederacy* without a fight in April 1781. He was paroled almost immediately to Norwich. He invested in one privateer and commanded another and again was captured and paroled. Harding then returned to the merchant service after the war, with a stint in prison for his debts, but he was too old and ill to continue for long. Impoverished, he and his wife relocated to New York and ran a boardinghouse catering to New England travelers and Connecticut's delegates to Congress. His applications for a pension went unanswered until 1807—twenty-four years after the war's conclusion. He died seven years later.[204]

Esther Smedley died in 1792 at the age of forty-one. She is an invisible presence in Smedley's life; any letters she wrote to her husband, if not lost on *Defence*, were consumed by the fires in 1779. She willed all of her property to her husband.

Samuel Smedley died on June 13, 1812, aged fifty-nine years, and was buried the following day beside his father. His estate tallied more than

Captain Samuel Smedley was buried next to his father, James. Today the gravestone of the great sea captain, privateer and customs collector lies broken and illegible. *Jackson Kuhl.*

$17,000. Smedley bequeathed money to nieces and nephews, and gave his half sister, Mary Beers, a $50 per year stipend along with all of "My land at Compo"—Compo Beach—which he had inherited from his wife. And this: "I give to the indigent of the town of Fairfield $200 to be distributed by my executors according to their discretion."[205]

And again Smedley demonstrated his deep internal embrace of American ideals. "Having given my negro boy Boston his freedom, a workshop & established him in his trade as a shoemaker," Smedley wrote, "I give him one thousand dollars to be paid him by my executors." Smedley also gave Boston's father, York, "whom I heretofore emancipated," a stipend of thirty dollars a year for the rest of his life. He then reimbursed the town "all which the said town may have paid for the support of Old Dick a negro man belonging to the estate of my brother John Smedley dec'd."[206]

One other person is mentioned in Smedley's will. "My watch which in a former will since destroyed I gave to my friend John Wasson since dead I now give to his eldest son," he wrote. John Wasson was his old shipmate from *Defence* and *Hibernia*.[207]

Five days after Smedley died, the United States plunged over the precipice into another war with Britain. If his opinions of the time reflected those of his neighbors, as they had during the Revolution, then Smedley felt much less enthusiasm for this conflict. Smedley had fought the American Revolution because he and most of Fairfield conceived of a world where they could pursue their business—support themselves, put food on their families' tables—free of the cumbersome taxes and restrictions of a government three thousand miles away. But Jefferson's Embargo Act and Madison's war were just as obstructive to Connecticut's shipping, if not more so. Often Smedley chided those whose commitment to liberty did not rise to his own. In respect to maritime commerce, even presidents failed him.

But between the wars were three decades of peace in which Samuel Smedley lived the second half of his life. He had endured screaming cannonballs, sickness, privation, arson, shipwreck and imprisonment for his reward. "Amidst the Greatest of Troubles & Difficultys of the World," Samuel Smedley wrote to Governor Trumbull in April 1778, describing the smallpox outbreak onboard *Defence* and the subsequent capture of *Cyrus*, "I find there is at Times some Pleasure."[208]

NOTES

1. "TWO CAN PLAY AT THIS GAME"

1. Boardman, *Log-Book*, 51–54; Coggins, *Ships and Seamen*, 65–78; Hawkes, *A Retrospect*, 67–69 (quotations); and John Torrans to Joseph Trumbull, June 3, 1778, Jonathan Trumbull Papers (hereafter JTP), vol. 8, part 1, 118.
2. Federal Writers' Project, *Connecticut*, 139 (quotation).

2. "A CONNECTICUT MAN BORN"

3. Jacobus, *History and Genealogy*, vol. 2, part 2, 796–97; Wheeler, *The Journal*, 25 (quotation).
4. Jacobus, *History and Genealogy*, vol. 2, part 2, 880–881.
5. Town of Fairfield in account with Samuel Smedley, April 1775, Revolutionary War Series 1 (hereafter RWS1), 32, 282.
6. Banks, *This Is Fairfield*, 52, 55.
7. Samuel Bradley, et al., to Samuel Smedley, October 28, 1786, Fairfield Museum and History Center (hereafter FMHC), Smedley Family Papers, MS 37, box III, folder Q; John Smedley to Samuel Smedley,

October 1787, FMHC, Smedley Family Papers, MS 37, box III, folder Q; Avitable, "Connecticut Overseas Trade," 178–79.

8. Commager and Cantor, eds., *Documents of American History*, 32–34, 38–39; McClellan, *Smuggling in the American Colonies*, 12–14, 20, 34–38; Wood, *The American Revolution*, 13.

9. Avitable, "Connecticut Overseas Trade," 180–82 (statistics); McClellan, *Smuggling in the American Colonies*, 38.

10. McClellan, *Smuggling in the American Colonies*, 43 (quotation).

11. Avitable, "Connecticut Overseas Trade," 177; Joseph Avitable, personal communication, January 25, 2011.

12. Commager and Cantor, eds., *Documents of American History*, 42–43.

13. Ibid., 32–34.

14. Lathrop, *Black Rock*, 6–8, 142–44 (quotation); Jacobus, *History and Genealogy*, vol. 2, part 1, 66–68; map of Andrew Skinner, FMHC, map 190.

15. Samuel Smedley to Peter Colt, March 31, 1787, Connecticut Historical Society (hereafter CHS), Jeremiah Wadsworth Correspondence, box 138, folder 2 (quotation).

16. Commager and Cantor, eds., *Documents of American History*, 53–55.

17. Hoadley, ed., *The Public Records of the Colony*, vol. 12, 410, 411 (quotation), 420–425.

18. Commager and Cantor, eds., *Documents of American History*, 63–64, 71–72, 76–78; Wilson, *History of Fairfield*, 281 (quotation).

3. "For the Defence of the Sea-Coasts"

19. Hoadley, ed., *The Public Records of the Colony*, vol. 15, 99–100, 111, 131.

20. Ibid., vol. 15, 176 (quotation), 201–02.

21. Ibid., vol. 15, 109, 200–01 (quotation); Goldsmith-Carter, *Sailing Ships*, 98–99.

22. Hoadley, ed., *The Public Records of the Colony*, vol. 15, 119, 200, 259; Coggins, *Ships and Seamen*, 16.

23. Middlebrook, *History of Maritime*, vol. 1, 45–47.

24. Ibid.; Naval Committee to the Virginia Convention, December 1775, *Letters of Delegates to Congress*, vol. 2, 544.

25. Commager and Cantor, eds., *Documents of American History*, 60–61; Hoadley, ed., *The Public Records of the Colony*, vol. 12, 451–53.
26. Collier, "The Revolutionary Privateers," 6.
27. Hoadley, ed., *The Public Records of the Colony*, vol. 15, 244–45 (quotation); Howard, *Seth Harding*, 3–6.
28. Hoadley, ed., *The Public Records of the Colony*, vol. 15, 229, 232, 236 (quotation).
29. Ibid., vol. 15, 245, 254.
30. Ibid., vol. 15, 259; *History and Genealogy*, vol. 2, part 2, 905.
31. Howard, *Seth Harding*, 10; Hoadley, ed., *The Public Records of the Colony*, vol. 15, 259.
32. Howard, *Seth Harding*, 12–13; Coggins, *Ships and Seamen*, 27–30; Hoadley, ed., *The Public Records of the Colony*, vol. 15, 262 (quotation).
33. Hoadley, ed., *The Public Records of the Colony*, vol. 15, 259; Seth Harding to Jonathan Trumbull, May 16, 1776, JTP, vol. 4, part 1, 87.
34. Seth Harding to Jonathan Trumbull, May 16, 1776, JTP, vol. 4, part 1, 87.
35. Todd, *The History of Redding*, 75–79; Howard, *Seth Harding*, 19–20.
36. Bookbinder, *Long Island*, 64–65; Flick, *Loyalism in New York*, 96–98 (quotation).
37. Hoadley, ed., *The Public Records of the State*, vol. 1, 158–159 (quotations).
38. Lamont, *The Story of Shelter Island*, 20 (first quotation); Bookbinder, *Long Island*, 72 (second quotation).
39. Seth Harding to Jonathan Trumbull, May 16, 1776, JTP, vol. 4, part 1, 87.
40. Seth Harding and Jonathan Sturges to Jonathan Trumbull, May 15, 1776, JTP, vol. 4, part 1, 87 (first and second quotation); Seth Harding to Jonathan Trumbull, May 16, 1776, JTP, vol. 4, part 1, 88 (third quotation).
41. Seth Harding to Jonathan Trumbull, May 16, 1776, JTP, vol. 4, part 1, 87 (first quotation), 88 (second quotation).
42. Howard, *Seth Harding*, 15, 20–21, 23–24.
43. Seth Harding to Jonathan Trumbull, May 20, 1776, JTP, vol. 4, part 1, 92 (first and second quotation); Seth Harding to Jonathan Trumbull, May 16, 1776, JTP, vol. 4, part 1, 87 (third quotation); Hoadley, ed., *The Public Records of the Colony*, vol. 11, 355.

44. Seth Harding to Jonathan Trumbull, May 20, 1776, JTP, vol. 4, part 1, 92; Seth Harding to Jonathan Trumbull, May 16, 1776, JTP, vol. 4, part 1, 87 (quotation).

45. Seth Harding to Jonathan Trumbull, May 16, 1776, JTP, vol. 4, part 1, 88; Hoadley, ed., *The Public Records of the Colony*, vol. 15, 486–487 (quotations).

46. Howard, *Seth Harding*, 20, 26–27.

47. Affidavit of Samuel Smedley, July 17, 1776 in Force, ed., *American Archives*, 402; Howard, *Seth Harding*, 3; Butterfield, ed., *Adams Family Correspondence*, 13–16 (second quotation).

48. Abigail Adams to John Adams, June 17, 1776, *Adams Family Correspondence*, 13–16 (quotations).

49. Ibid.

50. Samuel Smedley to Jonathan Trumbull, June 20, 1776, JTP, vol. 5, part 1, 102 (quotations); Abigail Adams to John Adams, June 17, 1776, *Adams Family Correspondence*, 13–16.

51. Seth Harding to Jonathan Trumbull, June 19, 1776, JTP, vol. 5, part 1, 93 (quotations); Samuel Smedley to Jonathan Trumbull, June 20, 1776, JTP, vol. 5, part 1, 102; Abigail Adams to John Adams, June 17, 1776, *Adams Family Correspondence*, 13–16; Cotton Tufts to John Adams, June 17, 1776, *Adams Family Correspondence*, vol. 2, 17–19.

52. Seth Harding to Jonathan Trumbull, June 19, 1776, JTP, vol. 5, part 1, 93 (quotation).

53. Hoadley, ed., *The Public Records of the State*, vol. 1, 578; Samuel Smedley to Jonathan Trumbull, June 20, 1776, JTP, vol. 5, part 1, 102 (first quotation); Seth Harding to Jonathan Trumbull, June 19, 1776, JTP, vol. 5, part 1, 93 (second quotation); Abigail Adams to John Adams, June 17, 1776, *Adams Family Correspondence*, 13–16.

54. Howard, *Seth Harding*, 32–36, 44–45; Cotton Tufts to John Adams, June 17, 1776, *Adams Family Correspondence*, 17–19 (quotation).

4. "To Cruise Against the Enemies"

55. Seth Harding to Jonathan Trumbull, June 27, 1776, JTP, vol. 5, part 1, 99 (quotation).

56. Seth Harding to Jonathan Trumbull, June 19, 1776, JTP, vol. 5, part 1, 93; John Bradford to Jonathan Trumbull, June 20, 1776, JTP, vol. 4, part 2, 121; Howard, *Seth Harding*, 39–42.

57. Howard, *Seth Harding*, 39–42; Holbrook, *Ethan Allen*, 113–31.

58. List of articles taken in the transports, July 27, 1776, JTP, vol. 5, part 1, 128.

59. Samuel Smedley to Jonathan Trumbull, June 20, 1776, JTP, vol. 5, part 1, 102 (first quotation); Ebenezer Bartram to Jonathan Trumbull, July 14, 1776, JTP, vol. 4, part 2, 139 (second quotation); Seth Harding to Jonathan Trumbull, June 27, 1776, JTP, vol. 5, part 1, 99 (third quotation); Samuel Eliot to Jonathan Trumbull, July 8, 1776, JTP, vol. 4, part 2, 137 (fourth quotation).

60. Clark, *Naval History*, 143; Howard, *Seth Harding*, 43; Samuel Eliot, Jr. to Jonathan Trumbull, January 22, 1779, JTP, vol. 9, part 1, 19 (quotation).

61. John Bradford to Jonathan Trumbull, June 20, 1776, JTP, vol. 4, part 2, 121 (quotations).

62. John Bradford to Jonathan Trumbull, June 23, 1776, JTP, vol. 5, part 1, 95 (first quotation); Seth Harding to Jonathan Trumbull, July 1, 1776, JTP, vol. 5, part 1, 104 (second quotation).

63. Samuel Eliot to Jonathan Trumbull, July 8, 1776, JTP, vol. 4, part 2, 137 (quotation).

64. Howard, *Seth Harding*, 46–47 (quotation and excerpt).

65. Holbrook, *Ethan Allen*, 114–15.

66. Ebenezer Bartram to Jonathan Trumbull, July 14, 1776, JTP, vol. 4, part 2, 139; Hoadley, ed., *The Public Records of the Colony*, vol. 15, 478–79 (quotation).

67. Coggins, *Ships and Seamen*, 26–27.

68. Ibid.

69. Howard, *Seth Harding*, 47.

70. Hoadley, ed., *The Public Records of the Colony*, vol. 15, 490–91.

71. Ibid., vol. 15, 504.

72. Ibid., vol. 15, 494–95 (quotations), 504.

73. Ibid., vol. 15, 513; Hoadley, ed., *The Public Records of the State*, vol. 1, 384 (quotation). Neither the old *Defence* (*Lily Ann*) nor the new *Defence* (*Endeavour*) should be confused with an unrelated third vessel, the *Defence* of Beverly, Massachusetts, which sank during the 1779 Penobscot expedition and was

excavated from 1975 to 1981 by the Institute for Nautical Archaeology, the Maine Maritime Academy and the Maine State Museum.

74. Hoadley, ed., *The Public Records of the Colony*, vol. 15, 499 (quotations).

75. Howard, *Seth Harding*, 49–50.

76. Hoadley, ed., *The Public Records of the State*, vol. 1, 53, 73, 87.

77. Howard, *Seth Harding*, 49–50.

78. Caulkins, *History of New London*, 516–21; Decker, *The Whaling City*, 44–48.

79. Hoadley, ed., *The Public Records of the State*, vol. 1, 84–85.

80. *Journals of the Continental Congress*, vol. 6, 913 (quotation).

81. Seth Harding to Jonathan Trumbull, December 12, 1776, RWS1, IX, 85 (quotations); Hoadley, ed., *The Public Records of the State*, vol. 1, 156.

82. Seth Harding to Jonathan Trumbull, December 21, 1776, RWS1, IX, 86 (quotations).

83. Seth Harding to Jonathan Trumbull, January 8, 1777, RWS1, IX, 87; Peters, ed., *New Medicine*, 302–04; McGrew, *Encyclopedia of Medical History*, 116–18 (quotation).

84. Seth Harding to Jonathan Trumbull, RWS1, IX, 87 (quotations).

85. Hoadley, ed., *The Public Records of the Colony*, vol. 1, 156 (first quotation); Seth Harding to Jonathan Trumbull, RWS1, IX, 90 (second quotation).

5. "MR SMEDLEYS BEHAVIOR"

86. Samuel Eliot to Jonathan Trumbull, March 16, 1777, RWS1, IX, 97 (quotation).

87. Samuel Eliot to Jonathan Trumbull, April 14, 1777, RWS1, IX, 99 (quotation).

88. Samuel Smedley to Jonathan Alden, March 22, 1777, RWS1, IX, 98 (quotation).

89. Samuel Eliot to Jonathan Trumbull, April 25, 1777, RWS1, IX, 102 (quotation).

90. Hoadley, ed., *The Public Records of the State*, vol. 1, 83–84; Caulkins, *History of New London*, 524–26; Samuel Smedley to Jonathan Trumbull, April 19, 1777, RWS1, IX, 101 (quotation).

91. Samuel Eliot to Jonathan Trumbull, March 16, 1777, RWS1, IX, 97 (quotations).

92. Samuel Smedley to Jonathan Alden, March 22, 1777, RWS1, IX, 98; Samuel Smedley to Jonathan Trumbull, April 19, 1777, RWS1, IX, 101.

93. Samuel Smedley to Jonathan Trumbull, April 19, 1777, RWS1, IX, 101; Samuel Smedley to Jonathan Alden, March 22, 1777, RWS1, IX, 98 (quotation).

94. Samuel Eliot to Jonathan Trumbull, April 25, 1777, RWS1, IX, 102 (quotations).

95. Hoadley, ed., *The Public Records of the Colony*, vol. 15, 200 (quotation).

96. Hoadley, ed., *The Public Records of the State*, vol. 1, 156 (quotation); Lamont, *The Story of Shelter Island*, 24–25; Middlebrook, *History of Maritime*, vol. 1, 212.

97. Hoadley, ed., *The Public Records of the State*, vol. 1, 213, 320, 343.

98. Samuel Smedley to Jonathan Trumbull, April 19, 1777, RWS1, IX, 101 (quotation).

99. Hoadley, ed., *The Public Records of the State*, vol. 1, 319 (quotation).

100. Samuel Smedley to Jonathan Trumbull, April 19, 1777, RWS1, IX, 101 (quotation).

101. William Coit to Jonathan Trumbull, February 24, 1777, RSW1, IX, 131 (quotation).

102. Jonathan Trumbull to Samuel Eliot, August 26, 1777, RWS1, IX, 187 (first quotation); Samuel Eliot to Jonathan Trumbull, September 10, 1777, RWS1, IX, 188 (second and third quotation); Hoadley, ed., *The Public Records of the State*, vol. 1, 399; Account of Ship Defence to Saml. Eliot Jr., August-December 1777, RSW1, IX, 246.

103. Samuel Smedley to Jonathan Trumbull, February 12, 1778, JTP, vol. 8, part 1, 75 (quotations).

104. Samuel Eliot Jr. to Jonathan Trumbull, May 10, 1777, RSW1, IX, 107 (quotations).

105. Samuel Smedley to Jonathan Trumbull, February 1777, RSW1, IX, 93; Henry Billings to Jonathan Trumbull, February 8, 1777, JTP, vol. 6, part 1, 33 (quotations).

106. Samuel Eliot, Jr. to Jonathan Trumbull, October 11, 1777, RWS1, IX, 204 (first and second quotations); Hoadley, ed., *The Public Records of the State*, vol. 1, 464 (third quotation).

107. Hoadley, ed., *The Public Records of the State*, vol. 1, 566 (quotation).

6. "A WARM COMBAT INSUED"

108. Samuel Smedley to Jonathan Trumbull, no date [1778], RSW1, IX, 248 (quotations).

109. Ibid.

110. Fenn, *Pox Americana*, 15–20; McGrew, *Encyclopedia of Medical History*, 313–17.

111. Fenn, *Pox Americana*, 33; McGrew, *Encyclopedia of Medical History*, 313–17.

112. Hoadley, ed., *The Public Records of the Colony*, vol. 15, 478–79 (quotation).

113. Ibid., vol. 11, 358–60 (first quotation); Schenck, *The History of Fairfield*, 206; Hoadley, ed., *The Public Records of the State*, vol. 1, 180–81 (second quotation). For examples of amateur inoculation in Fairfield, see *The Journal of William Wheeler*.

114. Hoadley, ed., *The Public Records of the State*, vol. 1, 206, 387, 401, 464.

115. Samuel Smedley to Jonathan Trumbull, no date [1778], RWS1, IX, 248 (first quotation); Timothy Parker to Jonathan Trumbull, April 20, 1778, RSW1, IX, 249 (second quotation).

116. Samuel Smedley to Jonathan Trumbull, no date [1778], RWS1, IX, 248 (quotation); Hawkes, *A Retrospect*, 68.

117. Hawkes, *A Retrospect*, 68 (first quotation); Samuel Smedley to Jonathan Trumbull, no date [1778], RWS1, IX, 248 (second quotation).

118. Hawkes, *A Retrospect*, 68 (quotation).

119. Samuel Smedley to Jonathan Trumbull, no date [1778], RWS1, IX, 248 (quotations); Hoadley, ed., *The Public Records of the State*, vol. 2, 101.

120. Timothy Parker to Jonathan Trumbull, April 20, 1778, RSW1, IX, 249 (first and third quotation); Boardman, *Log-Book*, 52 (second quotation).

121. Timothy Parker to Jonathan Trumbull, April 20, 1778, RSW1, IX, 249 (quotations).

122. Timothy Parker to Jonathan Trumbull, April 20, 1778, RSW1, IX, 251 (first and second quotations); Boardman, *Log-Book*, 53 (third quotation).

123. Rose & Torrans to Joseph Trumbull, October 13, 1778, JTP, vol. 8, part 2, 208 (quotation).

124. Rose & Torrans to Joseph Trumbull, June 3, 1778, JTP, vol. 8, part 1, 118 (first and second quotations); Samuel Smedley to Jonathan Trumbull, August 3, 1778, in Middlebrook, *History of Maritime*, vol. 2, 312–13 (third and fourth quotations).

125. Rose & Torrans to Joseph Trumbull, June 26, 1778, JTP, vol. 8, part 2, 149 (quotations).

126. Hawkes, *A Retrospect*, 70 (quotation).

127. Ibid., 70–71 (quotations).

128. *The Gazette of the State of South Carolina*, June 24, 1778 (quotation).

129. Hawkes, *A Retrospect*, 71 (first quotation); Rose & Torrans to Joseph Trumbull, June 26, 1778, JTP, vol. 8, part 2, 149 (second quotation).

130. Rose & Torrans to Joseph Trumbull, June 26, 1778, JTP, vol. 8, part 2, 149 (first quotation); Rose & Torrans to Joseph Trumbull, August 15, 1778, JTP, vol. 8, part 2, 174 (second quotation).

131. Hoadley, ed., *The Public Records of the State*, vol. 2, 167 (first quotation); Rose & Torrans to Joseph Trumbull, August 15, 1778, JTP, vol. 8, part 2, 174 (second quotation); Rose & Torrans to Joseph Trumbull, October 13, 1778, JTP, vol. 8, part 2, 208 (third quotation); Rose & Torrans to Joseph Trumbull, April 28, 1779, JTP, vol. 9, part 2, 192 (fourth quotation).

132. Timothy Parker to Jonathan Trumbull, July 17, 1778, CHS, American Revolution Collection (1776–1786), box AMREV/1776-10, folder 10A (quotation); Boardman, *Log-Book*, 63–68.

133. Hawkes, *A Retrospect*, 71–72.

134. Samuel Smedley to Jonathan Trumbull, September 17, 1778, JTP, vol. 8, part 2, 184 (quotations).

135. Timothy Parker, et al. to Jonathan Trumbull, January 6, 1779, JTP, vol. 9, part 1, 2 (quotations).

136. Samuel Smedley to Nathaniel Shaw Jr., December 15, 1778, New London County Historical Society, Nathaniel and Thomas Shaw Papers, microfilm, reel 2, 412 (first quotation); Thomas Cable to Nathaniel Shaw, Jr., January 25, 1779, CHS, American Revolution Collection (1776-1786), box AMREV/1776-10, folder 10C (second and third quotations).

137. Report of committee inquiry into state and circumstances of *Oliver Cromwell* and *Defence*, January 1779, RSW1, XIII, 359 (quotations);

Assembly resolution regarding *Oliver Cromwell* and *Defence*, no date, RSW1, XIII, 360.

138. Hoadley, ed., *The Public Records of the State*, vol. 2, 215–16 (quotations).

139. Samuel Smedley to Jonathan Trumbull, March 12, 1779, JTP, vol. 9, part 1, 95 (quotations).

140. Ibid.

141. Nathaniel Shaw to Jonathan Trumbull, March 13, 1779, JTP, vol. 9, part 1, 102 (quotations).

7. "The Flames Have Now Preceded Your Flag"

142. Samuel Smedley to Jonathan Trumbull, March 12, 1779, JTP, vol. 9, part 1, 95 (quotations).

143. Bill for Court of Enquiry Capt. Smedly, March 17, 1779, RSW1, XIV, 51.

144. Samuel Smedley to Jonathan Trumbull, March 20, 1779, JTP, vol. 9, part 1, 112.

145. Hoadley, ed., *The Public Records of the State*, vol. 2, 218, 354; Middlebrook, *History of Maritime*, vol. 1, 125–26.

146. Hoadley, ed., *The Public Records of the State*, vol. 2, 122–24 (first quotation); Samuel Squire et al. to Jonathan Trumbull, July 2, 1779, JTP, vol. 9, part 2, 260 (second and third quotations).

147. Samuel Squire et al. to Jonathan Trumbull, July 2, 1779, JTP, vol. 9, part 2, 260 (quotations).

148. Ibid.

149. Ibid.

150. Ibid.

151. Goodrich, "Invasion of New Haven," 53 (quotation).

152. Ibid., 67–82 (quotation).

153. Ibid., 87–91.

154. Hurd, ed., *History of Fairfield County*, 283–84 (quotation); Hoadley, ed., *The Public Records of the Colony*, vol. 15, 240–41.

155. Hurd, *History of Fairfield County*, 283–84 (quotation).

156. Ibid.

157. Ibid.

158. Schenck, *The History of Fairfield*, 386–87 (quotation).

159. Ibid.

160. Ibid., 431 (quotation).

161. Ibid., 430 (quotation). There were several women named Mary Beers at the time. This may be Smedley's half sister, Mary, wife of Reuben Beers.

162. Ibid., 432 (quotations).

163. Ibid., 434 (quotation).

164. Wheeler, *The Journal*, 30 (first quotation); Hurd, *History of Fairfield County*, 284 (second quotation).

165. Wheeler, *The Journal*, 30 (first quotation); Schenck, *The History of Fairfield*, 433 (second and fourth quotations); Hurd, *History of Fairfield County*, 284 (third quotation).

166. Hurd, *History of Fairfield County*, 284 (first quotation); Wheeler, *The Journal*, 30 (second and third quotations).

167. Wheeler, *The Journal*, 30.

168. Ibid., 30–31 (quotations).

169. Ibid., 31 (first quotation); Shepard, "David Barlow" (second quotation).

8. "To Keep Body & Soul Together"

170. Burnett, ed., *Letters of Members*, 401.

171. *Journals of the Continental Congress*, vol. 4, 251–54 (quotation).

172. Clark, *Naval History*, 133–40; *Journals of the Continental Congress*, vol. 4, 251 (quotation) and vol. 9, 792; Hoadley, ed., *The Public Records of the Colony*, vol. 15, 262.

173. Middlebrook, *History of Maritime*, vol. 2, 194–203 (quotation).

174. Ibid., vol. 2, 194–203; Dan Scovell to E. Hallam, March 31, 1780, JTP, vol. 11, part 1, 124 (quotation).

175. Middlebrook, *History of Maritime*, vol. 2, 194–203 (quotation).

176. Ibid.

177. Ibid., vol. 2, 200 (quotation); Coggins, *Ships and Seamen*, 79–84.

178. Middlebrook, *History of Maritime*, vol. 1, 40–41 (first and second quotations); Wheeler, *The Journal*, 32–33 (third and fourth quotations), 36.

179. Dan Scovell to E. Hallam, March 31, 1780, JTP, vol. 11, part 1, 124 (quotations); Robinson, *The Hazard Family*, 68–69.
180. William Greene to Jonathan Trumbull, April 18, 1780, JTP, vol. 11, part 2, 143 (quotation).
181. David Sproat to Col. Ledyard, May 11, 1780, JTP, vol. 11, part 2, 180 (quotation).
182. Middlebrook, *History of Maritime*, vol. 2, 127 (first and third quotations); Esquemeling, *The Buccaneers*, 189 (second quotation).
183. Middlebrook, *History of Maritime*, vol. 2, 123–25; *The Pennsylvania Packet*, September 4, 1781, JTP, vol. 23, part 2, 201.
184. Middlebrook, *History of Maritime*, vol. 2, 130–31 (first quotation); *The Connecticut Gazette and the Universal Intelligencer*, December 19, 1780, JTP, vol. 23, part 2, 171 (second quotation).

9. "SAMUEL SMEDLEY OF CONNECTICUT RAN AWAY"

185. "The Old Mill Prison," 19–21.
186. Maclay, *A History*, 149–51.
187. Middlebrook, *History of Maritime*, vol. 2, 325; Bowman, *Captive Americans*, 52–54.
188. Middlebrook, *History of Maritime*, vol. 2, 325 (quotation).
189. Sparks, ed., *The Diplomatic Correspondence*, 243–44 (first quotation); Wharton, ed., *The Revolutionary Diplomatic Correspondence*, 37 (second quotation). For a full description of Franklin's efforts to relieve American sailors, see Clark's *Ben Franklin's Privateers*.
190. Maclay, *A History*, 152–55.
191. Middlebrook, *History of Maritime*, vol. 2, 325 (quotation).
192. Sparks, ed., *The Diplomatic Correspondence*, 246–48 (quotations).
193. Ibid.; Wharton, ed., *The Revolutionary Diplomatic Correspondence*, 37 (first quotation) and 159–60 (second quotation).
194. Thomas Barclay to Benjamin Franklin, April 11, 1782, Papers of Benjamin Franklin (hereafter PBF), vol. 37, 134 (quotation).
195. David Salisbury Franks to William Temple Franklin, December 23, 1781, PBF, vol. 36, 36.289a002 (quotation).

196. Wharton, ed., *The Revolutionary Diplomatic Correspondence*, 542 (quotation).
197. Thomas Barclay to Benjamin Franklin, April 25, 1782, PBF, vol. 37, 213; Thomas Barclay to Benjamin Franklin, April 29, 1782, PBF, vol. 37, 237 (quotation).
198. Thomas Barclay to Benjamin Franklin, June 17, 1782, PBF, vol. 37, 493 (first quotation); Thomas Barclay to Benjamin Franklin, June 27, 1782, PBF, vol. 37, 560 (second quotation).
199. Wharton, ed., *The Revolutionary Diplomatic Correspondence*, 720 (quotation).

10. "Amidst the Greatest of Troubles"

200. Washington, *The Diaries*, 21–23 (quotation).
201. Ibid.
202. *Naval Records*, 393; Collier, "The Revolutionary Privateers," 24–25.
203. *Naval Records*, 423, 456; Collier, "The Revolutionary Privateers," 68–69.
204. Howard, *Seth Harding*, 145–94.
205. Will of Samuel Smedley, March 17, 1812, Fairfield Probate Office, Fairfield Probate Records 1795–1821, vol. 28, 263–64 (quotations).
206. Ibid. Boston took Smedley's surname. In October 1821, Boston's wife, Dorcas, died at the age of thirty of puerperal fever, a kind of sepsis that can occur during childbirth or miscarriage; there's no mention of a child in the records. Three years later, Boston married Mathilda Berlin in the Congregational church.
207. Ibid.
208. Samuel Smedley to Jonathan Trumbull, no date [1778], RSW1, IX, 248 (quotation).

BIBLIOGRAPHY

American Revolution Collection (1776–1786). Connecticut Historical Society, Hartford, Connecticut.

Avitable, Joseph. "Connecticut Overseas Trade, 1640–2009." *Connecticut History* 49, no. 2 (Fall 2010): 176–86.

Banks, Elizabeth V.H. *This Is Fairfield, 1639–1940*. New Haven, CT: Walker-Rackcliff Co., 1960.

Boardman, Timothy. *Log-Book of Timothy Boardman*. Albany, NY: Joel Munsell's Sons, 1885.

Bookbinder, Bernie. *Long Island: People and Places Past and Present*. New York: Harry N. Abrams, Inc., 1983.

Bowman, Larry G. *Captive Americans: Prisoners during the American Revolution*. Athens: Ohio University Press, 1976.

Burnett, Edward C., ed. *Letters of Members of the Continental Congress*. Vol. 1. Washington, DC: Carnegie Institution of Washington, 1921.

Butterfield, L.H., ed. *Adams Family Correspondence*. Vol. 2. Cambridge, MA: Belknap Press of Harvard University Press, 1963.

Caulkins, Frances Manwaring. *History of New London, Connecticut*. New London, CT: H.D. Utley, 1895.

Clark, Thomas. *Naval History of the United States*. Vol. 2. 2nd ed. Philadelphia, PA: M. Carey, 1814.

Clark, William Bell. *Ben Franklin's Privateers*. Baton Rouge: Louisiana State University Press, 1956.

Coggins, Jack. *Ships and Seamen of the American Revolution*. Harrisburg, PA: Stackpole Books, 1969.

Collier, Thomas S. "The Revolutionary Privateers of Connecticut." *Records and Papers of the New London County Historical Society*. Part 4, vol. 1. New London, CT: New London County Historical Society, 1893.

Commager, Henry Steele, and Milton Cantor, eds. *Documents of American History*. Vol. 1. 10th ed. Englewood Cliffs, NJ: Prentice Hall, 1988.

Decker, Robert Owen. *The Whaling City: A History of New London*. Chester, CT: Pequot Press, 1976.

Esquemeling, John. *The Buccaneers of America*. New York: Charles Scribner's Sons, 1893.

Federal Writers' Project of the Works Progress Administration for the State of Connecticut. *Connecticut: A Guide to Its Roads, Lore, and People*. Cambridge, MA: Riverside Press, 1938.

Fenn, Elizabeth A. *Pox Americana: The Great Smallpox Epidemic of 1775–82*. New York: Hill and Wang, 2001.

Flick, Alexander Clarence. *Loyalism in New York During the American Revolution*. New York: AMS Press, 1970.

Force, Peter, ed. *American Archives*. Series 5. Vol. 1. New York: Johnson Reprint Co., 1972.

The Gazette of the State of South Carolina, June 24, 1778.

Goldsmith-Carter, George. *Sailing Ships and Sailing Craft*. London: Hamlyn Publishing Group Ltd., 1969.

Goodrich, Reverend Chauncey. "Invasion of New Haven by the British Troops, July 5, 1779," in *Papers of the New Haven Colony Historical Society*. Vol. 2. New Haven, CT: New Haven Colony Historical Society, 1877.

Hawkes, James. *A Retrospect of the Boston Tea-Party, with a Memoir of George R. T. Hewes, a Survivor of the Little Band of Patriots Who Drowned the Tea in Boston Harbour in 1773*. New York: S.S. Bliss, Printer, 1834.

Hoadly, Charles J., ed. *The Public Records of the Colony of Connecticut*. Vols. 10–15. Hartford, CT: Case, Lockwood & Brainard Co., 1877–1890.

———, ed. *The Public Records of the State of Connecticut*. Vols. 1–2. Hartford, CT: Case, Lockwood & Brainard Co., 1894–1895.

Holbrook, Stewart H. *Ethan Allen*. Portland, OR: Binford & Mort Publishing, 1988.

Howard, James L. *Seth Harding, Mariner*. New Haven, CT: Yale University Press, 1930.

Hurd, D. Hamilton, ed. *History of Fairfield County, Connecticut, With Illustrations and Biographical Sketches of Its Prominent Men and Pioneers*. Philadelphia, PA: J.W. Lewis & Co., 1881.

Jacobus, Donald Lines. *History and Genealogy of the Families of Old Fairfield*. Vol. 2, part 1–2. Baltimore, MD: Genealogical Publishing Co., 1991.

Jeremiah Wadsworth Correspondence. Connecticut Historical Society, Hartford, Connecticut.

Jonathan Trumbull Papers. Vols. 4–23. 1776–1781. Connecticut State Library, State Archives, Hartford, Connecticut.

Journals of the Continental Congress, 1774–1789. Vols. 4–9. Washington, D.C.: Government Printing Office, 1906.

Lamont, Helen Otis. *The Story of Shelter Island in the Revolution*. Shelter Island, NY: Shelter Island Historical Society, 1975.

Lathrop, Cornelia Penfield. *Black Rock, Seaport of Old Fairfield, Connecticut, 1644–1870*. New Haven, CT: Tuttle, Morehouse & Taylor Co., 1930.

Maclay, Edgar Stanton. *A History of American Privateers*. London: Sampson Low, Marston & Co. Ltd., 1900.

McClellan, William S. *Smuggling in the American Colonies at the Outbreak of the Revolution with Special Reference to the West Indies Trade*. New York: Moffat, Yard and Company, 1912.

McGrew, Roderick E. *Encyclopedia of Medical History*. New York: McGraw-Hill, 1985.

Middlebrook, Louis F. *History of Maritime Connecticut during the American Revolution, 1775–1783*. Vols. 1–2. Salem, MA: Essex Institute, 1925.

Nathaniel and Thomas Shaw Papers. Microfilm. New London County Historical Society, New London, Connecticut.

Naval Records of the American Revolution, 1775–1788. Washington, D.C.: Government Printing Office, 1906.

"The Old Mill Prison, Plymouth, England." *Magazine of History* (January 1915).

Papers of Benjamin Franklin. Digital edition (franklinpapers.org). New Haven, CT: American Philosophical Society, Yale University and Packard Humanities Institute.

Peters, David, ed. *New Medicine Complete Family Health Guide*. London: Dorling Kindersley, Ltd., 2005.

Revolutionary War Series 1. Microfilm. Connecticut State Library, State Archives, Hartford, Connecticut.

Robinson, Caroline E. *The Hazard Family of Rhode Island, 1635–1894*. Boston: self-published, 1896.

Schenck, Elizabeth Hubbell. *The History of Fairfield, Fairfield County, Connecticut, From 1700 to 1800*. Vol. 2. New York: self-published, 1905.

Shepard, Betty. "David Barlow, the 'ci devant' farmer." *Town Crier*. March 25, 1965.

Skinner, Andrew. Map 190. Fairfield Museum and History Center, Fairfield, Connecticut.

Smedley Family Papers. MS 37, box III, folder Q. Fairfield Museum and History Center, Fairfield, Connecticut.

Smedley, Samuel. Will. Fairfield Probate Records 1795–1821. Vol. 28. Fairfield Probate Office, Fairfield, Connecticut.

Smith, Paul H., et al., eds. *Letters of Delegates to Congress, 1774–1789*. Vol. 2. Washington, D.C.: Library of Congress, 1976–2000.

Sparks, Jared, ed. *The Diplomatic Correspondence of the American Revolution*. Vol. 3. Boston, MA: Nathan Hale and Gray & Bowen, 1829.

Todd, Charles Burr. *The History of Redding Connecticut*. Newburgh, NY: Newburgh Journal Company, 1906.

Washington, George. *The Diaries of George Washington, 1748–1799*. Vol. 4. Cambridge, MA: Riverside Press, 1925.

Wharton, Francis, ed. *The Revolutionary Diplomatic Correspondence of the United States*. Vol. 5. Washington, D.C.: Government Printing Office, 1889.

Wheeler, William. *The Journal of William Wheeler*. Reprinted in Cornelia Penfield Lathrop, *Black Rock, Seaport of Old Fairfield, Connecticut, 1644–1870*. New Haven: Tuttle, Morehouse & Taylor Co., 1930.

Wilson, Lynn Winfield. *History of Fairfield County, Connecticut, 1639–1928*. Vol. 1. Hartford: S.J. Clarke Publishing Co., 1929.

Wood, Gordon S. *The American Revolution*. New York: Modern Library, 2003.

INDEX

V

W

ABOUT THE AUTHOR

Jackson Kuhl is a writer, photographer and historian. His work has appeared in the *Hartford Courant, Connecticut Magazine, Fairfield County Weekly* and elsewhere. More of his writing and photos can be found at jacksonkuhl.com.

Visit us at

www.historypress.net